MELD AND EGON

MELD AND EGON

A Way Out of America's Political Dementia

Kenneth E. Willis

iUniverse, Inc.
New York Lincoln Shanghai

MELD and EGON
A Way Out of America's Political Dementia

iUniverse, Inc.

For information address:
iUniverse, Inc.
2021 Pine Lake Road, Suite 100
Lincoln, NE 68512
www.iuniverse.com

ISBN: 0-595-26922-2

Printed in the United States of America

"Society is produced by our wants, and government by our wickedness; the former promotes our happiness positively by uniting our affections, the latter negatively by restraining our vices."

—Thomas Paine

CONTENTS

▼

ABOUT AMERICA'S GOVERNMENTS

"A government by the passions of the multitude, or no less correctly, according to the vices and ambitions of their leaders, is a democracy. We have heard so long of the indefeasible sovereignty of the people, and have admitted so many specious theories of the rights of man, which are contradicted by his nature and experience, that few will dread at all, and fewer still will dread as they ought, the evils of an American democracy."

—**Fisher Ames** (1758–1808)

Americans must love government since they have so much. Every town, city, county and state has a government overlaid by a gigantic federal authority. Since political leaders are elected, there can be little doubt that America's love affair with government grows. Everyone complains about overgrown and ineffective government, but the complaints are usually couched in terms of "why doesn't the government do something about......?" Yet there is no serious political movement dedicated to reducing the size of government. Institutions such as Cato, Reason and the Heritage are laying intellectual foundations for halting government's growth, but this foundation has no structure.

Big government cannot exist without politicians who advocate and support government's growth. While some consider politics an honorable profession, most citizens know that politicians are a deceptive and smarmy lot. There is no punishment for politicians who fail to meet their commitments. Politics is the only profession immune from the law of contracts. Other personal characteristics, such as honesty and rationality, could not survive the electoral contest. Citizens want to hear sweet lies about what their politician will do for them once elected, even though they know it won't happen.

There are some citizens who really don't like government. Libertarians and "militias" are sincere in their contempt for government and consistently advocate reducing the size and authority of the federal government. These groups are a tiny minority and are likely to remain so, especially as an ever-increasing number of citizens receive financial aid or services from government to which they have become dependent, and possibly addicted.

America was established as a Republic, not a Democracy. The Founding Fathers provided a constitution that defined the architecture of a Republic that has functioned very well over the years. The intention was clearly to emphasize civil society and minimize the role of government in the lives of the citizens. Now our governments consume an ever-increasing portion of a growing American economy. While America's governments are not as expensive as Europe's in terms of percent of gross national product, the absolute magnitude of resources consumed by American governments exceeds that of any other nation. Having observed the destructive effects of large and omnipotent governments in other countries, Americans should pause and think before embracing their own mega-governments.

Governments create social structures. The result is not a "zero sum game." There is no pot of wealth and happiness available for distribution among the citizens. The amount of wealth a society creates is dependent on incentives created by the laws. Citizen's happiness is determined primarily by their wealth and the freedom to do as they please. If the incentives created by the laws become perverse, the creation of wealth slows and civility is replaced by policing. America's

Republic served its citizens well for over 200 years, it should surprise no one that some fine tuning is in order after monumental changes in demographics and technology.

Is it possible to restore a government of consensus and legitimacy to America? This analysis starts with the assumption that a good government strives for *legitimate consensus* and fosters an environment of *creating* rather than *taking*. By using a rational approach to defining government, this book describes the essential elements of a good government, and equally important how to implement a system of good government. The first step is to create a consistent vocabulary. Politicians, academics and newscasters have trashed the vocabulary of politics and political science. They redefine words used to express political concepts in order to render the noxious palatable. Politicians are horrified that citizens will learn the true nature of government. The images provided by civic texts and Fourth of July speeches better serve the deception. Governments *are simply* associations *that declare their exclusive* right *to use* force *to make their members obey the rules of the* association.

Political and academic elite now dominates America's governments. Tom Sowell coined the term "anointed ones" to describe this group. The anointed cling to power by encouraging trivial conflicts among citizens and pleading for "compassion" to justify increasing government control. Achieving consensus and an environment of creating rather than taking is not in the anointed's interest; they maintain power by redistributing wealth and encouraging meaningless conflict. If the thirst for power and wealth were the anointed's only sins, the cost would be tolerable. Unfortunately they do much greater harm by creating laws and regulations that are superficially planned, based on intuition or the pseudo-science of their bureaucrats and often result in the exact opposite of the proclaimed effect. These laws wreak economic and personal disasters. The politicians encourage debate over irrelevant issues as a distraction from their agenda to seize power and transfer wealth. This is not a new theme in human history, but one that America hoped it left behind. Unfortunately, this is not the case.

A legitimate government with broad consensus must be based on *principles* that are not easily compromised. The principles cannot be perverted to suit the whims of a majority of citizens, the judiciary, the president or the legislature. The *social* contract embodied in the American constitution gives preference to *civil* society over *political* society. Strict limits on the role of government are defined. The constitution preserves the principles that achieve consensus. Any social compact that achieves broad consensus must be limited in scope. Consensus does not mean everyone agrees with every government action; it means that the citizens accept the rule of law as the best compromise between unfettered freedom and protection from their fellow citizens. Modern technology and demographic realities have a significant impact on the construction of a workable government. The constitutional safeguards that preserve negative law must be strengthened. *Negative* law defines what citizens *may* do; *positive* law what they *must* do.[1] A legitimate and workable government must have consistently enforced negative laws and few positive laws.

The purpose of this book is to define new government architecture. This government is derived from *axioms* that require *consensus* and *creating* rather than *conflict* and *taking*. The primary role of the national government is enforcing negative law. Positive law originates at the lower levels of political jurisdiction, the city, county or state. The "supreme" court is restricted to enforcing constitutional constraints on governments, associations and citizens (the *negative* law). *Positive* law is approved by electronic voting methods available to all citizens. Citizens

---

1. as pointed out by F. A. Hayek "*That practically all rules of just conduct are negative in the sense that they normally impose no positive duties on any one, unless he has incurred such duties by his **own** actions, is a feature that has again and again, as though it were a new discovery, been pointed out, but scarcely ever systematically investigated.*"

may vote positive law issues directly, or join associations that cast votes for them. Instead of two political parties, citizens can join multiple associations that reflect their values, and cast their votes on issues related to the interests of the association. Alternatively, they can study the issues and cast their vote electronically from their home or workplace. Longer periods of time are allowed for decision-making. Anyone is free to spend their own resources to campaign for or against a positive law. This method of democratically creating positive law is totally practical with modern telecommunications and data processing technology. A computer system records all votes and is maintained by an elite civil service. The role of the politician is substantially reduced.

Alternatives offer little hope. Democracies degenerate into issue driven, majority dominated societies that practice destructive zero-sum behavior. Authoritarian governments suppress freedoms, destroy wealth creation and aggrandize a few at the expense of many. The Republic worked well in America for over 200 years. The politicians now in charge are intent on accumulating power and wealth at the expense of productive citizens. The anointed's stranglehold on our governments is made possible by modern communications and transportation technology and the bounty of our productive industries. It is time these tools were used to make government better serve the interests of citizens rather than the "anointed."—**There is a better way.**

▼

DO YOU LIKE YOUR *GOVERNMENT?*

"That one human being will desire to render the person and property of another subservient to his pleasures, notwithstanding the pain or loss of pleasure which it may cause to that other individual, is the foundation of government."

—John Stuart Mill

"Government is not reason, it is not eloquence. It is force. Like fire, it is a dangerous servant and a fearsome master."

—George Washington

—a brief history of government

A few hundred thousand years ago two cave dwellers, Haag and Aaag, went hunting. As they trudged along, Haag started complaining about the Clan Leader, who he contended was doing crazy things and was not fit for leadership. "For example," he said, "last winter, we found an intruder, nearly frozen, outside the cave. The leader insisted that we bring the intruder into the clan and provide food and skins. We barely had enough food for ourselves. All the women objected. As you well know, the women are a majority of the clan members. The intruder should have been killed on the spot." Aaag thought for a moment and then responded "I'll admit the Leader has been a bit off the wall lately, but I think bringing the intruder into the clan was a smart move. The clan needs to grow. Our numbers have been diminishing lately. The intruder has paid her way. She taught us how to sharpen our hunting sticks on a rough stone and harden them over the fire. It's been easier to kill the tigers since then." Haag shot back, "That's another thing that makes me mad, the Leader is now making everyone sharpen the hunting sticks; I don't like anyone telling me how to hunt." Aaag responded, "Well if you feel strongly about it there are the clan rules. You can challenge the Leader to a fight to the death, and then kill the intruder yourself—if you win. You could also leave and form your own clan; if you can find a cave and get anyone to join. Finally, you can shut up and keep hunting. If you don't start killing more meat than you eat, the Leader may kick you out of the clan." As they saw the shadow of a tiger ahead, Haag mumbled "I'll put up with it for now, but I am mad as hell and I am not going to take it anymore."

More recently two farmers sit at a bar in Oklahoma. Jake said to Hovey," this new guy Roosevelt has gone crazy; he is taking our tax money and giving it to those unemployed guys in New York City. If they had stayed on the farm where they belong, they wouldn't be unemployed and we wouldn't have a depression." Hovey responded "I think he's doing the right thing, the whole country has to get back to work before any of us will be better off. Besides, I like what I've been hearing about this new parity thing for wheat price supports. Those bastards down at the grain elevator won't pay enough for my crop to cover the damned mortgage." As Jake finishes his beer and moves off the bar stool, he mutters "shouldn't let people farm if they do not have enough money to buy the land."

A few decades later two stockbrokers, Sid and Marvin are eating lunch at a Manhattan deli. Sid complains, "those nuts in congress are spending billions to bail out the S&L's. Most of the bastards who are in trouble were crooks anyway, and now they are tapping into my wallet to pay off the fools who put their money into CD's instead of buying stocks." Marvin agreed, saying that congress was incredibly stupid to increase deposit insurance while removing any restrictions on how the deposits are invested. They called it "de regulation" when they meant a "license to steal." On the other hand, once it happened, it was probably smart to prop up the financial system. If that much liquidity had been drained out overnight a lot of people would have sold their stocks, crashed the market and we would be out of a job." Sid finishes his corned beef and mutters, "I think the damned legislators who voted for Garn-StGermaine should be put in jail." "So do I" says Marvin.

These examples of political debate are repeated every day, from the local bar to the halls of academe and the chambers of congress. No resolution was reached between Haag and Aaag, and none have been reached at Harvard or in Washington. The idea of limiting government actions against citizens matured with the Magna Carta and the American Bill of Rights. Constraints on government actions against their citizens are a new development in human society. As the idea of limiting government matures, public debate focuses on whether a government should undertake so many responsibilities. Governments may have overgrown, if not outlived, their usefulness.

—how governments get that way

Many individuals have vested interests that are best served by large governments; particularly those whose jobs depend upon government. These government sycophants try to divert the debate away from whether their jobs are necessary and focus on what their jobs should entail. Public sector unions have demonstrated that bureaucrats are remarkably tenacious in protecting their jobs. Government jobs always provide greater security and more generous pay and benefits than jobs in civil society. Bureaucrats focus their energy on preserving their jobs and benefits. Productive citizens are too busy to effectively oppose these groups.

The catastrophic failures of central government planning should cause the advocates of expansive government to have second thoughts. Nothing could be further from the truth. These well-documented failures do not diminish the enthusiasm of collectivists in the least. The Soviet Union provided a grand social experiment in government planning. The results are evident. American advocates of expanded roles for government are numerous and loud. Only in countries governed by fundamentalist religious orders or despots is there a greater dedication to empowering the "leaders" to define correct behavior. As the debate about the *value* and proper *role* of government evolves, intellectual, economic and political resources are brought to bear. Legions of PhD's, ex-statesmen, retired generals, and successful businesspersons are being organized into think tanks, political action groups, round tables, conferences and fund raising events. These groups present evidence; analysis and anecdote that proves governments are either good or bad. What motivates such intense interest in these subjects?

Governments degenerate to grand Ponzi schemes. The modern "Ponzist" government collects some wealth from the victims (citizens) with a promise of returns far beyond reasonable expectations. A portion of this wealth is redistributed to the victims. This process generates no new wealth. As collections from new participants are distributed to earlier participants the illusion of enormous wealth creation appears. The idea is so pleasant that none of the participants want to challenge the concept. The victims are now convinced of the soundness of the promises made by the perpetrator, so another round of "contributions" follows. The cycle repeats until the arithmetic of collection and redistribution collapse. If the society is growing in population and wealth, the inevitable collapse is postponed.

Participants in these political debates cross traditional party lines. "Liberals" contend government is good but needs reforming, while "conservatives" espouse the evils of government but behave quite the contrary. As Michael Stern points out in "Beyond Left and Right", both liberals and conservatives divide into "order" and "freedom" camps. This division better describes attitudes toward government. The "order" camp can manifest itself as extreme environmentalists or the religious fundamentalist opposing abortion; groups not generally considered political bedfellows. The common bond is that both groups want the government to impose an agenda that logic and persuasion are not sufficient to carry. The "freedom" camp wants to minimize government's authority over the individual. Political labels become meaningless. Citizen's values become more diverse as options are made available by technology and increased wealth. A political party's platform cannot embrace a diversity of values that will appeal to a majority of citizens.

Modern politicians rarely take a definite position on important issues. Politicians and bureaucrats recognize government as their employer; they never bite the hand that feeds them. Citizens find that government enhances neither their ideology nor material needs. The citizen's view of the politician is increasingly hostile. The politician's view of the citizen is cynical and totally lacking respect. Geingus Kahn had more respect for his subjects than a typical congressman.

The constituent of an elected government is self-serving; not altruistic. This constituent will not be critical of the government if he perceives his needs are being served. If a warlord in Mogadishu provides food to his subjects they are certain to overlook his propensities to atrocity, corruption and megalomania. The key word is "perceived." An adroit politician can convince citizens that black is white, that suffering is good for them, that their benefactor is a thief or that without the politician's protection they would perish. Religious or nationalistic leaders convince otherwise sensible people that dying (now) is good for them.

The intellectuals and politicians know that voters are dim-witted and self-serving. As the economists say, these citizens have a high discount rate. They do not pay much attention to the future and do not base their votes or decisions on the long haul. This kind of decision maker, according to the politician, is the greatest danger to democracy. The politician asks, "What does it take to convince the citizen that he needs the government to decide how he spends his money and his life?" Politicians know that only the government can take the 'long view' and save the world for our grandchildren. This pseudo-altruism ensures employment for the selfless politicians, supporting bureaucrats and a cadre of sycophant lawyers and academics. Because of this alleged short-sightedness of citizens, we cannot be surprised at any action the ungrateful constituents might undertake, from bombing a federal building to voting for Ross Perot.

The most respected and highly trained minds endlessly debate the value and proper role of government. Why is it not possible for an assemblage of great intellectuals, such as that convened in the Congress of the United States of America, to reach consensus on the proper role of government? Why does congress divide itself into two teams that pretend to oppose each other? This behavior is more consistent with a kindergarten class than a political assembly. Each issue should be debated on its merits. Votes could be cast without adherence to vaporous and indistinguishable party lines. There is little in the behavior of these "distinguished gentlemen" to merit the citizen's respect or even tolerance.

—let us reason together.

The language and logic used in political "science" does not work. Science unleashed the secrets of the atom, discovered DNA, invented the airplane and explained the origin of the universe. Organizing society to be productive and non-destructive remains unaccomplished. Is rationality and logic a useful tool? Is it necessary to settle ideological differences by conflict? Is any consensus permanent, or does human DNA contain the seeds of conflict? Is democracy a flawed concept because the tyranny of the majority (or the special interests supposedly representing the majority) will prevail? Has political consensus of the "new world order" been achieved, or is this an illusion created by the order imposed by the military superiority of America and the ex-USSR? Will it be possible for the world's poor to grow richer through effective governments and free trade, or must they be doomed to the basement of society under the guise of protecting the environment and American jobs?

The recent collapse of the USSR has precipitated debate about the role and value of government. The ex-Soviet Union experienced severe economic problems. This situation was greeted with relish by a number of western politicians and analysts. With expressions of vindication and self-righteousness, these observers pronounce that the fate of the USSR demonstrates the superiority of democracy and capitalism over communism and economic planning. There is an element of truth in these observations, but they seriously oversimplify the lessons learned from the plight of the Russians and their ex-republics. More seriously, this over-simplified analysis obscures many problems that are evolving in "democratic" governments. These problems parallel the real causes of the Soviet collapse. American politicians and bureaucrats have exhibited neither moral nor intellectual superiority over their Soviet counterparts.

Central economic planning cannot provide economic efficiency. The use of synthetic prices and bureaucratically planned resource allocations has serious shortcomings. It is particularly difficult to implement such a scheme without powerful data processing and data collection tools. The USSR had neither. Widespread corruption in the government caused serious misapplication of resources. Citizens lacked confidence in the government. These situations led to low worker morale and reduced productivity. Chernobyl and the Aural Sea demonstrate how government planning leads to ecological disasters. The militaristic discipline imposed by economic planners prevented middle level managers from taking initiatives to solve production and logistics problems. A distorted system of rewards caused massive falsification of performance records. This resulted in an inaccurate picture of managers' performance. The biggest lie garners the greatest reward. Much of the economic performance information, readily available in the West, was guarded by the paranoid planners. People who needed this important data were denied access. The government planners could not tell the good guys from the bad guys. The obvious inequities in rewards versus performance demoralized the entire work force. An old Russian joke sums up the experience: "We pretend to work and they pretend to pay us." The bright spot in the Soviet system was education; emphasis was placed on science, reasoning to solve problems and the English language. This undoubtedly contributed to the downfall of the communists. America's government run educational system is making no such mistake. In Russia, the return to popularity of the communists is predominantly among the older and rural citizens; those not exposed to the formal educational system put in place by the USSR.

American and most Western European governments call themselves democratic. They define their economies as either "free market" or "mixed." Unless these words are interpreted loosely, both statements are misleading. More important, "democracy" does not create success in the production of goods and the satisfaction of citizens' values. Many trends now evident in America and Europe are leading to the same political scenario that destroyed the Soviet Union. Political leaders intentionally obfuscate these issues because they benefit from the expansion of government. To sort out the valuable lessons from the hyperbole, it is necessary to determine real cause and effect, not attribute the Soviet's problems to inadequate ideology.

If governments are to learn from past mistakes, they must understand the underlying causes of their failures. Attributing problems to ideological deficiencies explains nothing. Authoritarian, centrally planned social structures can evolve slowly; they do not have to be born by revolution. America's political emergence two centuries ago was a unique event. The American concept has been transplanted and copied, but never duplicated. Age seems to have destroyed America's ability to sustain those safeguards so essential to a free and healthy civil society.

If a new political technology is to work, it must implement a new paradigm more effectively than existing governments perpetuate themselves. This is no small task. This must be accomplished without loosing control of the process and generating a worse situation. Vested interests are waiting like vultures to find ways to transfer government-confiscated wealth to themselves. Entire industries have evolved for the sole purpose of capturing wealth the government confiscates and then transfers to those deemed meritorious. These vested interests now have substantial resources and associations with the political process that will be difficult to disconnect. It is easier to define a better government than to implement one. Bovard's "Lost Rights" explains why.

Citizens become increasingly dependent upon the wealth redistributed by the all-powerful government. They lose the will and the resources to resist the confiscation of their earned wealth. Just as in the USSR, Iraq and North Korea, the citizens come to the horribly mistaken belief that the government is the source of wealth. The citizens believe the government must be paid homage if they are to receive a pittance in return for their efforts. This political Ponzi scheme has worked well in the past, but one would hope that modern America is more sophisticated than to let it happen here. All evidence points to the contrary.

—why are we so confused?

The Gordian knot of modern political debate can be unraveled by understanding two phenomena:

1. Language—Political debate uses language as the primary tool of deceit. Deceptive language is a short cut to capturing the minds and hearts of citizens when facts, logic and reason either proves too cumbersome or demands the opposite of the proposition. Most of the words used in the political and social science literature are meaningless. The current academic fads of "deconstruction", "relativism" and "political correctness" are aimed precisely at the destruction of reason and logic as society's tools of social organization and economic progress. Achieving effective communications requires a consistent vocabulary that everyone can comprehend and use in meaningful discourse. Words that describe *concepts* rather than *objects* are particularly vulnerable to subtle redefinition. If newscasters suddenly started calling an apple an orange, everyone would immediately notice and judge them mad. But when a word like freedom or democracy is slowly twisted to mean different things in different contexts, no one thinks it odd. The purpose of debate is to disclose disagreements of facts or values. If participants in the debate can agree on their disagreements they may find more common ground than expected. The sophistic, divide and conquer tactics of the modern demagogue or political science professor prevent effective communication. The liberal media's slavish adoration of these "anointed ones" further compounds the confusion.

2. Human Behavior—Does social conditioning or heredity drive human beings to polarized ideological positions? Why do violent religious or nationalistic governments become so expansive and parochial? Similar forces are at work in the minds of citizens in modern, liberal societies. An explanation of the origin and behavior of government requires an understanding of citizen's values. The behavior observed in Bosnia and Rwanda is not that different from south LA. Civility is a thin veneer over the brutal and aggressive human animal. The Rouseauian concept of an inherently good "noble savage" is totally contradicted by the facts. (See Steven Pinker's "The Blank Slate—the Modern Denial of Human Nature.") The ugly side of human behavior must be fully accounted for in a government that provides stability and

protects its citizens from fraud and aggression by fellow citizens (particularly their leaders).

It is difficult to remain objective when analyzing governments. Stalinists were not eager to hear countervailing theories to Lyshenkov. American political advocates are no more enthusiastic about facts and logic that debunk their dogma. A level of irrationality comparable to Lyschenkov is found in America today. The apocalyptic environmentalists preach that the end is near unless their political prescriptions are followed. Politically Correct zealots demand the end to free speech and equal outcomes in all human competitions. The "annointed's" refusal to accept any role for genetics in determining social outcomes is Lyshenkovianesk. American political discourse is overwhelmed with dogma and does not address real issues and real alternatives.

A language useful for analyzing governments must use words that avoid emotion-laden responses. Building a vocabulary, syntax and logical structure for the analysis of government comes first. Our inability to achieve political consensus is buried in millennia of mental wiring diagrams that favor one or another approach to social organization. These human attributes undoubtedly had significant survival value at some time and place. In order to better explore this idea, new words are used to describe these social paradigms. The words are MELD and EGON. The definition of Meld and Egon are based on fundamental human attitudes toward social organization.

There *are* differences in citizens' values. This is not justification for the political elite to exploit these differences. While Meld and Egon battle over ideological issues, the vultures are running away with the resources of both. It is time to construct a government that will not result in vacuous debate and acrimony while the thieves are looting everyone who is productive. Politicians have played the equivalent game of setting the boarding house on fire in order to distract the sheriff while they rob the bank. The distraction is accomplished by focusing the citizen's attention on *taking* rather than *creating*. The result is a profitless zero-sum game. America must be restored to a society devoted to *consensus* and *creation*, not *conflict* and *taking*.

Political actions result from individual's values. If the purpose of a political act is to accomplish a goal defined by citizens' values, then it is important that the act have the desired result. Citizens do not benefit from politician's proclamation of success. Many of the perversions in our current political system parallels the Soviet's problems. Actions taken by the government lead to a result opposite from that proclaimed when the action was taken. This malfunction of the political process results from sloppy thinking, sophist presentations that hide the politician's real agenda, and unjustified exercise of government power to satisfy egos or vested interests. In this respect, America is becoming more like the USSR. Examples of inept legislation are federal deposit insurance to protect the "small saver", government "help" extended to native Americans, agricultural subsidies for the "small farmer", Aid to Families with Dependent Children and on and on.

A *science* of government would accurately predict the outcome of a government action. Governments always claim their actions are beneficial; they are usually destructive. Governments rarely meet their obligations; they simply consume and redistribute wealth. The damage done by governments portending to do good falls into one of three categories:

1. The purpose of the action is to satisfy a vested interest that will reward the politician, but that is not in the best interest of the citizen. The politician gives a reason for the action that is a lie. He knows what the outcome will be, but tell the citizens something else. An example is the marketing orders that limit fruit sales. The purpose is to maintain higher prices that benefit growers. The reason given for the action is to insure the highest quality fruit for the consumer. The net result is the transfer of wealth from consumers to growers. Every citizen is capable

of selecting his own oranges. The subsidies to ethanol producers provided under the guise of improving air quality and reducing dependence on foreign oil is a multi-billion dollar rip off that enriches many cooperative politicians.

2. The second type of misguided action results from stupidity. The initiators of the action did not analyze the situation carefully and predicted the wrong outcome. Most government miscarriages are of the first type since elected officials are not generally stupid; they are self-serving. Assuming Jim Wright and the banking committee were stupid and not criminal, the savings and loan fiasco provides an example of the second kind of error. Perhaps it was beyond the prescience of congress to realize that when financial executives were allowed to pay any rate of interest and invest other people's money as they chose, while the government *guaranteed* the principle, then legal theft was irresistible.

3. The third type of destructive action is the creation of laws that are contradictory. An example is legislation that spends public funds to campaign against tobacco consumption while maintaining generous price supports for tobacco farmers. Lawyers are endlessly enriched by contradictory legislation. When lawyers become judges they use these real or imagined inconsistencies to do their will. The Supreme Court has proven masters at this trade; witness the use of the commerce clause in the constitution to justify an intrusion by federal government into any private activity.

American political processes, from congress to the town council, have routinely practiced all of these techniques. Noxious addenda, added to the basic legislation and hidden from the public, compliment the deceit. The unnoticed addenda quietly gain the force of law. These hidden agendas, buried in hundreds of pages attached to the basic legislation, would cause an outcry if seen by the public. Often the legislators never review the hidden agenda before they vote. They base their decisions on special interest horse-trading without regard to the interests of citizens.

Governments have a profound tendency to run amuck as they age. Governments follow a life cycle similar to the individual human. In their prime governments are vigorous and effective. Effectiveness is not necessarily a blessing to the citizens if the government is ugly. In middle age governments become conservative and less creative, depending more on the habits and skills developed in youth. In old age they become senile and barely function. Then they die; sometimes slowly with a lingering ailment and sometimes swiftly from a massive malfunction. Some are early bloomers and some late bloomers. Some live short and violent lives and some become pleasant geriatrics. Modern technology impacts the life cycles of governments as much as it does individuals. New risks of sudden and violent death have emerged, but so have life saving methods. Modern communications and weapons technologies have extended the life of many senile governments.

Is this life cycle of governments inevitable? Could society devise a more stable and productive form of government? The introduction of every new "ism" claimed this solution was at hand—none have worked. The physical and biological sciences build on past discoveries to continuously improve control over nature. A science of government can effectively use these techniques.

▼

CHAPTER 2

SAY WHAT YOU MEAN—MEAN WHAT YOU SAY

"Power is in inflicting pain and humiliation.
Power is tearing human minds to pieces and putting them
together again in new shapes of our own choosing
Big brother is watching you
Newspeak
Doublethink
War is Peace
Freedom is Slavery
Ignorance is Strength"

—George Orwell

—modern politics

An elected politician faces an inquiring, scandal hungry press. He often finds himself between a rock and a hard place. His diverse constituents have many special interests. These interests are economic, ideological or the availability of infrastructure and services. The politician must win a majority of votes. Each group he addresses responds to the issues with a kaleidoscope of positions. In the good old days, party politics defined the agenda. The constituents would join the party and become part of a monolithic group. The voters cooperated by defining their interests consistent with the party. The politician could count noses and take the positions guaranteed to win. In this circumstance, his only challenge is to demonstrate greater sincerity in his commitments. This task better suits those who run for elected office. The diversity of interests and sources of information available in America now makes this strategy fail. If the candidate takes a definite stand on any significant issue, he is certain to irritate, if not alienate over half the voters. Any national politician who takes definite positions on abortion, gun control, school prayer and affirmative action will not be elected regardless of which side of the positions he is on. The elected official must follow three strategies if he is to win.

1. He must take definite positions only on *insignificant* issues. The constituents will not care about these issues. Even better, he can create new insignificant issues that he accuses others of opposing. He then convinces the voters that his position on the irrelevant issue is correct and important. The recent war on drugs is a masterful example of diversion from important issues with a non-issue. The enormous cost of this war will pale compared to the next irrelevant issue being prepared for the American citizen, the war on global warming.

2. When addressing substantive issues he must use words without meaning, words that have positive connotations, words that flow smoothly off the lip but can offend no one. No one could be opposed to a "Resolution Trust Corporation," a "safety net," a "deficit reduction," or for that matter, to "change." Such deceptive words either imply actions contrary to the intended ones or are meaningless and used to pretend there is a solution to a perceived problem.

3. Create animosities, or preferably hatreds, between two groups of citizens who can readily notice their differences (black versus white, poor versus rich, Catholic versus Protestant). After creating the conflict between the groups, the politician then sides with the largest group and denigrates the smaller, usually guaranteeing a majority of the vote. This trick can work even when the groups do not realize they have no reason to be in conflict Wars have been promoted to secure a political regime.

Political debate uses words that are carefully selected to be meaningless. Words are redefined to appear as a "solution" to a "problem." The word "contribution" is used to describe how citizens will pay for a government mandated health care scheme. Another example is the word "empowerment." The word implies that certain welfare recipients can take matters into their hands. The real meaning is that a congressional committee or cabinet executive will visit and let them complain for a few hours. The professional politicians have become so adept at the manipulation of words to hide their true agenda that the analysts, political science professors and newscasters are absorbed in the deceit. Academic amateurs tried to join the game by dictating Politically Correct speech to reform minds along an egalitarian agenda. The efforts were so transparent and un-professional that the cat was soon out of the bag. It is astonishing how quickly universities have abandoned first amendment rights in order to pursue egalitarian agendas. A former university president defended a group that destroyed 14,000 newspapers because they contained a politically incorrect editorial. This gentleman, who later became a high level federal official, said "Penn is not a public university and is thus not technically bound by the Bill of Rights." This poorly disguised attempt to mold opinion by speech coercion has outraged many sensible people. Success at the game of verbal deceit requires consummate skill and a big budget. Muddle headed professors cannot pull it off unobtrusively unless the victim is a mush mind product of modern American education.

—say what you mean and mean what you say.

Most words used to describe political, social and economic ideas must be abandoned. Examples include "conservative, liberal, communist, socialist, capitalist, natural rights, and freedom." The first step in analyzing governments is to define a vocabulary that is clear and precise. These definitions are provided in the Appendix. Subsequent discussions are limited to these words and other unambiguous elements of the English language. The goal is to provide a vocabulary of non-emotive words that allow all flavors of political persuasions to express fact or opinion in an understandable manner. The same vocabulary can be used to respond with equally understandable statements of opposing or confirming fact or opinion. Such techniques are successful in the sciences and mathematics. The anti-science Luddite may complain that a richness of language is lost through such procedures. This is irrelevant since the goal is to create a *science* of government, not a literature or art of government.

The analytical reader may prefer to go to the Appendix now and read the precise definitions of the politically active words that will be used in the rest of the book. The remaining contents will certainly make sense if the common associations are made, but some ambiguities may arise. If so, the reader can retire to the Appendix to clarify a particular word in question.

The next chapter uses these "clean" definitions to explain how governments are built and how they function. The structure, organization and behavior of governments have a profound impact on the extent to which citizens can realize their values. *The goal is to design a* government *that enhances the achievement of* citizens' values. Only then can a government be called "legitimate."

CHAPTER 3

▼

WHAT IS A GOVERNMENT?

"Physical violence is the basis of authority. Government is an association of men who do violence to the rest of us."

—Count Leo Nikolaevich Tolstoy

—say that again, Senator

Politicians distort the meaning of words. It is often impossible to understand what they are saying. This is particularly true of the labels they attach to their associations. The words Democrat, Republican, Socialist, Communist, Liberal, Conservative and Fascist all have emotion driven responses and imprecise meanings. A science of government cannot use words with such vague meaning.

These doublespeak labels were developed by politicians and are cultivated with discipline and enormous media expenditures. Civil society treats brand names such as Buick, Marlboro and Budweiser with great respect. Legal protection, and media exposure generates a larger market. Consumers spend more for these products. These words are given significant value, called "good will" by the accountants. Politicians generate and protect particular words or phrases in the same way, and unfortunately for more devious purposes. A science of government must develop a vocabulary that avoids such obfuscation.

Government is a unique kind of association. A government's charter claims the exclusive use of force for ensuring that the member's behavior is compliant with the charter. The government determines the time and extent of force needed. Force exclusivity precludes any resistance, even verbal, when a citizen is confronted with the government's demand for compliance. The definition of an association requires members to acknowledge their membership. The government uses force exclusivity to *define* its membership, and informs the members of their status after the fact. The member usually acknowledges such notification, in whatever form it arrives.

Force exclusivity may not be explicit in the law. Leaders never discuss the subject. The reality of force exclusivity is made clear by the presence of police, courts, jails and gas chambers.

—good guys and bad guys

Two associations with different charters may define their membership to overlap. War follows, either civil or international. Membership or charters must be resolved by force or negotiation. The result will be a single charter that defines the new association, or the original charters with non-overlapping membership.

When individuals challenge force exclusivity, governments react quickly. If an individual uses force for personal gain or pleasure it is termed "criminal." When charter issues are at stake, it is called "terrorism" or "treason." Challenges to the government's force exclusivity are met with the most severe punishments defined by the law. An example of this response was the Branch Dividian Cult exorcised in Waco, Texas by the Federal Bureau of Investigation and the Bureau of Alco-

hol, Tobacco and Firearms. The Dividian's only apparent infringement (initially) was the possession of some weapons the government
felt improper. An S&L executive that steals millions of dollars by fraud
receives mild if any punishment. The armed bank robber who steals a
few thousand dollars will spend years in jail. Governments have never
taken kindly towards challenges to their force exclusivity. Governments always exhibit enthusiasm for disarming their citizens, particularly when the citizen's enthusiasm for their government wanes.

The union is a quasi-government association that the government may
or may not tolerate. Unions can challenge government's force exclusivity. Modern societies incorporate into their charters assurances that
individuals own their effort. Slavery has been eliminated by laws if not
in practice. Associations called unions form to collectively negotiate a
price for the association members' labor. The controversial part of the
union's negotiating position is the strike, or the collective withholding
of labor. When bureaucrats form unions withholding individual member's labor (in a complex and interdependent economy) is an exercise
of force that challenges the government's force exclusivity. Collectively
withholding labor in a critical time or place meets the criteria for
applying force. In some governments, unions are not allowed at all
(that is, strikes are not allowed, even though the word union may be
used incorrectly). Governments will not allow disruption of their
agenda by citizens who withhold their labor. Non-government associations must deal with unions as they would with any provider of a commodity. Governments implement laws that define how negotiations
with unions are conducted. The most successful unions are those that
bargain for bureaucrats in nations that elect their leaders. The bargaining power of a union of bureaucrats is created through an implicit col-
lusion between the elected leaders who need votes and public sector
unions with the ability to deliver these votes. Private sector unions also
engage in bargaining with politicians for legal preferences in negotiating labor contracts. Private sector unions have not maintained member's voting discipline as effectively as the bureaucrat's unions. Unions

of bureaucrats have organized election fraud to assure the government remains sympathetic to their employment. A recent example was the teacher's union response to a California initiative to provide free choice for school attendance.

—the structure of government

A charter defines the structure of government. This structure impacts the satisfaction or thwarting of citizens' values. To understand how a government effects citizens' values, it is necessary to know how it is created and how it works. This process is described in four steps.

1. *staffing* a government is necessary to get it started, establish its force exclusivity and collect wealth.

2. The *functions* a government decides to perform are important in determining how much mischief it can do or prevent.

3. After committing to perform functions, the government must *organize* itself. Organization determines the effectiveness and efficiency of a government. Effectiveness is not necessarily a blessing to the citizens.

4. A government's *performance* can be measured. Performance measures will be used to design a good government.

STAFFING Much can be learned about governments by observing their staffing methods. A government conceived of but not properly staffed is just a bad dream. Staffing uses two categories of contract between citizens and the government. There are leaders and bureaucrats. Both are paid in cash or in kind by the use of force exclusivity. The association extracts their pay from member citizens by threatening force if payment is withheld. The leaders decide the level of pay for themselves and the bureaucrats.

Leaders are unique in their method of appointment. Bureaucrats are hired and fired by leaders or other bureaucrats empowered by the leaders to hire and fire. Leaders are appointed by one of three processes:

1. Self appointed.

2. Elected by a procedure and an electorate defined in the charter.

3. Succession by the rules of the charter. Succession can also be accomplished by force. A revolution can overhaul or suspend the charter and replace the leaders.

To simplify the description of Government Leaders And Bureaucrats (GLAB) an acronym for this group will be used to coin the word glab. This word will be used in the remainder of this book when referring to the leaders and staff of a government.

The privatization of public services is increasingly popular. Privatization avoids the coercion of public sector unions but confuses the issue of government staffing. A service contracted to a private sector individual or association and paid for by confiscated resources is still a government function. The firm's employees are not glabs. Alternatively, many functions the government has chosen to monopolize can be privatized; that is the services are made available by voluntary exchange. An example is the fire department that offers its services for an annual fee or for payment when called to fight a fire, but is privately established and funded. In this case the government chose to exclude the function of fire fighting from it's charter. Eliminating is preferable to privatizing a government function. When governments purchase commercially available goods and services, the sellers are not glabs.

Services are often declared "natural monopolies" by the government. This allows the glabs to create barriers to entry and sell, for cash or votes, the privilege to practice the monopoly. The "natural monopoly" argument is specious and self-serving. Examples include cable TV, telecommunications, the postal service and electrical power generation. Opening competition and assigning ownership rather than franchising or privately monopolizing the function would better serve citizens' interests.

Political effort is individual actions directed towards or resulting in a change in an association's charter or staffing. Political effort effects government and non-government associations. Positive law in the government's charter prohibits certain political activities, particularly those that would change the established government.

Individuals are most concerned with government political activity. Civil political activity is benign. Without the use of force a civil association's staff and charter are of little interest to non-members. Business enterprises may have conflicts among members to change the charter or the board members (leaders). This political activity is of little consequence to the typical citizen since the resulting decisions cannot be forced upon him.

FUNCTIONS The functions of government are the things they do. Organization determines how they are done. The following functions encompass most of the things governments can do. Government alone can accomplish some functions because these functions require force. Civil associations can perform other functions acquired by government since they do not require force exclusivity. Any function can be subject to government control, either exclusively (e.g. the postal service) or non-exclusively (e.g. a secondary home mortgage market). Government is the 600 pound gorilla; it sits where it wants. Functions that can only be performed by government because they require force are:

Police—Policing is the application of force to citizens by glabs. Force is an essential tool for government. Police do not threaten, they apply the force required to achieve immediate compliance. Deterrence is the mainstay of police activity since their numbers do not allow direct application of force for every infringement. If social structures become weak and the incentives for citizens to violate the charter become great, policing is difficult. Excessive positive law exacerbates the policing problem. The fewer positive laws, the fewer police required. This explains why police unions are generally in favor of any positive law; they are not conservative, just greedy. An effective, professional police will predict when instabilities arise, and notify their leaders. Corrective actions can range from providing food to public executions.

Judicial—The judiciary's primary function is to authorize the use of force by the police. Judges interpret law in order to force resolution of conflicts. The most important function of the judiciary is preventing glabs from creating law or administrative rulings in conflict with constitutional (negative) law. This function is seriously eroded in modern America. The second most important function is enforcement of contract law. The American judiciary performs this function reasonably well. The first function preserves civil society; the second prevents anarchy.

Inter-government relations establish workable interfaces between governments, negotiate international technical standards and manage war-making assets. Leaders often find irresistible the use of war making assets for domestic political control.

Executive—The executive manages, staffs and administers association functions. Empowering bureaucrats establish a hierarchy of authority.

Legislative—The legislature creates or changes positive law. The legislative function should be prevented from tampering with negative law at all costs.

Propaganda is government generated or sponsored data. Propaganda ranges from classroom education provided by government operated schools to raw statistical data collected by glabs. Regardless of the data's accuracy or origin, if it is disseminated by glabs, it is propaganda.

Regulation—Governments can require, under threat of force, individuals and associations behave in manners that are not in their best interests. Regulation is positive law. Regulation is not contract enforcement because the parties did not voluntarily commit to the obligation. Regulations may prohibit owning property or may require that resources be consumed in a manner not to the owners liking. Regulations are mandates. The government provides no compensation for loss of wealth or rights created by the regulation.

Redistribution—allocates confiscated resources or empowers enforcement of laws that effect transfer of wealth. Redistribution includes direct payment of money, provision of goods or services, guaranteeing loans and insurers, regulation or selective relief from taxation. Charity also redistributes wealth, but with the important caveat that the transfer is voluntary, not accomplished under the threat of force.

Creating constitutional law (the charter) Charters can evolve over a period of time, and then be adopted as a constitution by a government. Charters can be created out of whole cloth upon the creation of a new government. Although charters can be changed during a continuous government, this process is usually made difficult by the terms of the constitution. Severe political malaise or revolution usually accompanies a significant change in the charter.

A government must perform all of these functions. Each function can only be performed by an association that exercises force exclusivity. In the simplest governments, such as the small town sheriff or the chief of a tribe, a single individual can perform all of the functions, generally with the consent of most citizens.

Several other functions may be left to non-government associations or be adopted exclusively or non-exclusively in the government's charter. These "optional" functions are:

Money—defines, creates and/or establishes acceptability of tokens for individual and association economic transactions. Most governments have claimed the exclusive right to declare and create money in order to preserve their ability to tax through the printing of money. It is not necessary for the government to create money; non-government associations can provide this service. When a government establishes a central bank that can issue (print) currency, then provisions for deposit insurance and prevention of counterfeiting become essential to maintain faith in the government's printed money. International financial markets, where currencies are brokered and arbitraged, have weakened the ability of governments to dilute their currencies.

Enterprise—Government can include enterprise-enabling clauses in its charter. The government association can then engages in production, brokerage, arbitrage and fraud. One type of brokerage governments are particularly fond of is insurance underwriting, usually forcing the insured to subscribe and therefore enforcing a particular pool for risk sharing. (The role of government in risk abatement is treated in Chapter 8.) The enterprise of banking is attractive for government involvement since it provides an indirect mechanism for redistribution. The Marxist model of government controls all enterprise while the laissez faire model allows individuals to own enterprises. Governments have a strong influence on enterprise through various licensing and regulatory activities even when they do not directly participate.

ORGANIZATION

Governments organize themselves in many ways. Multiple governments can coexist in a hierarchy by structuring charters so they do not conflict. The overlapping charters can be structured so the staff and organizations of the governments are integrated. America has a robust hierarchy with national, state, county, township and or city, even borough or community government. This hierarchy is costly due to redundant and overlapping functions and staff. In America, state and local governments account for approximately 82,000 associations with 500,000 elected politicians (leaders) and over 13,000,000 employees (bureaucrats). This group of individuals represents a powerful coalition whose vested interests are served by expanding government. When the groups that depend on government contracts are included, the total exceeds 25% of the U.S. labor force. Add those who are dependent on government redistribution's (Social Security, Unemployment Compensation, AFDC, etc.) and the totals approaches 50% of the population. The dangers of this state of affairs in a democratic welfare state are obvious. Politicians covet this scenario since it guarantees control over citizens.

Governments complicate their organization through overlapping jurisdictions. A county, may overlap a city, a state, a federal government and a school district. Such inefficiency created by double staffing is justified under the rubric of 'checks and balances'. The real reason for multiple layers of government is to create jobs for glabs. It is rare to see a government jurisdiction dissolve itself, even after the justification for its existence has long passed. County governments continue to exist alongside city governments in areas where the city's growth has subsumed the county. Multiple levels of government act as an organism that coordinates an attack on citizens. The argument is often made that lower tiers of government are less oppressive, and hence better suited to serve their citizens. This is an illusion perpetrated by small politicians. Smaller units of government are part of the organism that oppresses all. Aside from occasional skirmishes, the multiple layers of government coordinate exquisitely in oppression of citizens.

As the hierarchy of government grows and becomes more complex, it is more difficult to avoid charter conflicts. This problem is particularly acute in America. The federal government requires actions by the states and cities that are expensive to implement. No funding is provided by the federal treasury to comply with the mandates. States and cities are adept at taxing and spending, but these additional fiscal burdens prove irksome. Federal law often overrides or contradicts local law.

PERFORMANCE

Most businesses, families and civil associations have measures of performance. Governments are seldom put to this test. Once a government is established, the next question is how it performs. From the citizen's point of view, the measures of performance are:

Consistency is essential if citizens are to respect the law. If the charter excludes some groups, usually glabs, from prosecution under the laws then citizens are alienated. Inconsistency in applying laws is disturbing for constituents. The practice of the Congress to exempt itself and its staff from constraining legislation is an example. Most governments practice some inconsistencies in applying laws. The leaders or privileged groups are often excluded. Affirmative action and subsidies to sugar farmers are as irritating to non-beneficiaries as are congressional rules that exclude glabs from prosecution.

Rights—Creation of rights and the vigor of the judiciary in enforcing them is a critical performance parameter. Negative law rights gain wider approval than positive law rights. Negative law rights define what an individual *may* do. Negative law rights were called "freedoms." The word "freedom" has recently been redefined to include positive law rights such as "freedom from poverty." For this reason the word was not included in the basic vocabulary. Positive law rights are defined by the citizen's access to goods and services or defines duties he must perform against his will. Since both positive law and negative law rights require the government to use force, rights only have meaning in the context of government. So called "natural" and "god given" rights have no meaning unless adopted by the governments charter and are, in this respect, indistinguishable from any other right.

Enterprise—Governments often include enterprise in their charter. Potential for mischief is much reduced if governments avoid enterprise. The Soviets dominated enterprise. The results of this grand experiment are well known. Governments have traditionally controlled or operated certain enterprises, but have left most to non-government associations. There are many reasons why governments always muddle attempts to operate enterprises. Wise authoritarian governments let civil society operate enterprises in order to maximize the wealth to be confiscated. Hitler's Germany was a good example of this practice. China's communists may have discovered this trick.

Stability—A beneficial or benign government that cannot survive is of little value. If citizens approve the functions government undertakes, society will be more stable. Stability can also be achieved with a strong police that suppresses dissent. Glabs can make the job of maintaining stability harder by prohibiting popular but unharmful activities. "Morality" laws grow from the need of politicians to find insignificant issues. Prohibitions often drive the forbidden activity underground and create a vicious circle of illegality, violence and greater crime than the forbidden activity. There is a delicate balance the well-intentioned government must achieve in defining rights and maintaining stability. A good government is useless if it is not stable. Bad government drives out good government, a process that has been proceeding in America for decades.

Inheritance—The right to inherit wealth is important to economic and family stability. The way governments treat the transfer of wealth upon the death of an individual has a major impact on stability and motivation. Inheritance policies can range from total confiscation of a deceased's wealth to applying a modest tax to the inheritors. No government has been able to tolerate the thought of confiscating no wealth at the time of death. Unless government can break all bonds of the family, inheritance laws will continue to have a strong influence on capital formation.

Money can be monopolized by government or provided by non-government enterprises. If government creates the money, then they can pay their bills by manipulating the money supply. A sensible government that monopolizes money will maintain stability in its value. This responsible approach has the noxious consequence of forcing the government to pay its bills through direct confiscation (taxes). Different ox's get gored depending on how this issue is handled. The rate of capital accumulation (savings) is strongly influenced by expectations of inflation and inheritance.

Ownership is the process of assigning wealth to individuals or associations. Governments use force to assure rules of ownership are respected. Some categories of ownership are reserved to the government. In the USSR individuals could only own goods. Government limits ownership by excluding certain real estate, the electromagnetic spectra or navigation rights from individual or non-government association ownership. Alternatively, governments can allow individuals to own all material and intellectual items with rules of achieving and sustaining ownership. *The major role government plays in avoiding anarchy is establishing and enforcing rules of ownership.* The most fruitful economic growth always occurs when governments minimized their ownership of goods, resources and enterprises and vigorously enforces consistent rules of civil ownership.

Ideology—Religious and nationalistic/jingoistic behavior can affect a government's performance. A government that includes ideological principles in the charter must allocate to a few glabs the task of translating these principles into actions. This is where the trouble begins. (This process can go very amuck as the Taliband demonstrated.)Some governments create their charter around ideological agendas; others maintain strict separation of ideology and the charter. "Moral" issues define how behavior prohibitions are compatible with tribal customs and collective behavior norms. These values may be important to a major segment of the association's members, and can have significant impact on maintaining social order. It is dangerous and foolish for a government to eradicate these constraints on behavior until they are sure the culture can survive without them. Social customs that are prohibited or diluted by the law can affect social stability. Enforcement (or lack thereof) of these norms can result in significant changes in individual behavior.

Fraud is associated with ownership. If ownership of wealth changes as a result of deception or a failure to meet contractual commitments, then fraud occurs. If a citizen violates a law that serves the government, mechanisms are always in place to remedy. If citizens engage in contracts and one of the parties violate the contract, who remedies the loss to the injured party? The government charter must take under its wing the resolution of private contractual disputes. An essential role of government is to provide a process for resolving contractual disputes. This function is necessary to avoid anarchy and encourage enterprise. Enterprise and voluntary contracts cannot flourish unless the parties are confident of protection against fraud. This protection can only be provided with the use of force. Italy and Russia are examples of how civil society degenerates when government *does not stop* fraud.

These issues summarize the functions and organization of governments. Citizens use these criteria to measure a governments' performance. This process implies no value judgments.

▼

CITIZENS

"I don't make jokes. I just watch the government and report the facts."

—Will Rogers

"Suppose you were an idiot and suppose you were a member of congress. But I repeat myself."

—Mark Twain

—is "good government" an oxymoron?

Why do governments exist? Are they necessary? Are they good? Can a society function without government? Government started with the first tribe or clan. The emergence of government in human societies seems as inevitable as maggots on a dog carcass. Can we predict or direct what kind of government evolves in a particular scenario? If citizens can control this process, what form of government should they seek?

An individual must have a value system in order to decide if a government is good. Until individuals define what they want out of life, it is difficult to determine whether a government is helping them accomplish their goals. For an individual, the task of defining his values may be harder than first appears; *primarily because we are accustomed to having government tell us what is good.* Governments provide an incessant stream of propaganda to advocate "good"; stop smoking, buy government bonds, join the Army, recycle trash and on and on. As knowledge and reasoning skills become more prevalent, it is harder for the government to establish values for citizens. Building pyramids and super-conducting super-colliders are examples of governments selecting activities that are "good" for us. Citizens are often unenthused about the "good" activity. A good government must consider individual's values when creating charters, organizations, functions and projects. Individuals have values; associations cannot. The relationship between government actions and citizen's values is the ultimate measure of performance. Individuals can have and express values that are irrelevant to governments. This list is pathetically short. America's federal government has perverted the "commerce clause" of our constitution to justify every conceivable intervention in civil society.

Politicians proclaim that their primary concern is enhancing the well being of their constituents. They lie. Their actions are quite the contrary. Leaders can be incompetent. They intend to achieve the well being of citizens, but somehow it just goes wrong and unintended outcomes prevail. Leaders are often self-serving and lie about the anticipated outcome. Leaders must recognize that the governed, if sufficiently provoked, can revolt. Revolts can have dire consequences for leader(s) as well as innocent bystanders. Albania provided a nice example.

A majority of citizens must remain productive if the government is to have sufficient wealth to confiscate. As manufacturing enterprises become more efficient, it is possible that over half the population is on the government payroll or dole. This is an unstable situation when leaders are elected and negative law is weak. If citizens elect their leaders, they can throw the bastards out. Unfortunately, voters are often duped by the sham of elections. If the alternatives presented to the electorate cannot change the performance of the government, then holding elections remedies nothing. Citizens are presented meaningless alternatives at elections while the politicians pretend the differences are critical. Democrats and Republicans recently displayed enormous differences over whether the budget should be balanced in 7 or 10 years! The bottom line is how well or poorly a government achieves the satisfaction of citizens' values, not how loudly the glabs proclaim success.

No circumstance or action can please all of the people all the time. The government's redistribution process can please those on the receiving end and displease those who are plundered. By some calculus of the "common good," the government concludes that their mission was successful; particularly if the redistribution keeps the leaders in power and avoids a revolution. When the government controls the redistribution process, the fox guards the chicken coop. For this reason, glabs should not be allowed to vote for leaders or on issues affecting their income or employment prospects. Passage of the Hatch Act was a major disservice to the nation.

When society perceives inequality in wealth, those on the lower end of the distribution will be pleased by equalization. If citizens have a more enlightened self-interest, they realize that the economy is not a zero-sum game. Inequalities in wealth can generate positive benefits far beyond the gains resulting from the egalitarian distribution of existing wealth. One of the greater ironies of a free society is that citizen's economic values are maximized when wealth distributions are skewed. The incentives inequalities provide are enormous. The popularity of lotteries indicates that individuals have no intrinsic repulsion to unequal distributions of wealth; in fact they relish it as long as they feel they can participate in the game on a level playing field. An elected politician's dream is a skewed distribution where a few have most of the wealth. The politician can then gain popularity by redistributing a small fraction of total wealth, thereby disrupting the wealth creation

process minimally. A closely related, and disgusting practice is for politicians to greatly exaggerate actual differences in wealth so they can
pander to greed by promising to tax the rich in a manner they deserve.
The politician is perfectly aware that pauperizing the top wage earners
would not make a dent in everyone else's wealth. In the last few years,
the top 5% of tax-payers paid 60 % of all income tax. Taxes are raised
on "the rich," but the poor never get richer. As egalitarian goals are
reached, it is increasingly evident that the overhead costs of running
the government are to everyone's detriment. The welfare states of
Scandinavian countries consume much of their wealth for government
overhead. The distribution of wealth in America is, contrary to public
perceptions, more egalitarian than most countries. The largest group of
owners of stocks and bonds are pension funds. Recently, the employees
gained a majority ownership of a major airline (and subsequently drove
it into bankruptcy). Social security obligations of the government command a substantial fraction of America's future wealth.

At the other end of the egalitarian spectrum is the despot who has a
strong police infrastructure and controls the source of wealth. He can
selectively redistribute wealth and enable bureaucrats, thereby maintaining stability while being niggardly with the citizens. The redistribution process is used to keep citizens powerless; if they do not obey they
do not eat. The inefficiencies of this process are irrelevant since the
purpose of the redistribution is to assure that everyone is dependent on
government. In governments where leaders are elected, the game is different. Such governments are euphemistically called democracies,
which is misleading since the citizens are not allowed to vote on any
issue that directly affects their values. Even in "democracies" the leaders show an enthusiasm for redistribution that far exceeds any desire for
"equality." A citizen dependent on government is less likely to revolt.
America's wealth redistribution programs are not motivated by altruism, but by the desire to cement control over the citizens. If this were
not true, there would be more poor beneficiaries of the redistribution.

A citizen may love his government as his favorite baseball team. Such affection will result in few demands as long as the government's image and rhetoric meet expectations. There are individuals who find no fault with their political party, football team or brand of beer regardless of the visible lack of meeting expectations. Political leaders seek this mind-set, or dogma. Irrational devotion to an image provides politicians with maximum flexibility and minimum exertion. These individuals are a politician's or a marketing executive's dream. If citizens understand how government manipulates them, then they will insist on full disclosure and the satisfaction of their values, not evasive rhetoric.

—*keeping score*

Government's performance must be scored by objective measures, not glab's proclamations of success. What criteria might we use? Government charters and actions should result in a substantial majority of shared values. If 90% of the citizens agree that their values are enhanced by an action, it would be a candidate for creating a government function. Protecting citizens from being murdered by foreign terrorists or foreign armies is a popular government activity. More mundane activities such as providing traffic signals and enforcing contracts probably score as well. There are many "no-brainers" that qualify for government involvement. If the extreme libertarian or anarchist protests that these activities can be provided by cooperative, voluntary associations, thereby avoiding the force exclusively clause in the charter, they are deluding themselves and nearing a full circle to communist ideology. Some citizens are nasty, mean and selfish (difficult to gratify). Government should not adopt an action or positive law opposed by a majority of the population. In all "democracies" much positive law created by the legislatures is opposed by a majority of citizens. Most positive law serves the interest of few citizens. Examples include agricultural subsidies, industrial regulations that limit competition, import tariffs, and thousands more.

Only individuals have values. Associations can advocate values, but values are relevant to government only as they influence individual efforts. Values are manifested in an individual through their efforts. Glabs have values, but they are in a privileged position to satisfy their values at the expense of other citizens. Individuals may dream or ponder alternate efforts, but until they apply effort to consume, create or advocate they have not expressed values. Values are manifested, measured and observed through individual efforts. Efforts by individuals are:

Type 1. Acts of consumption or creation that are for personal pleasure and have no impact on other individuals. Examples include, reading a book, consuming food, painting a picture, etc. Collectivists may contend that breathing air and consuming food has significant impact on others. This interpretation is nonsense. The individuals supposed to be affected are not aware of the harm done them.

Type 2. Acts engaged in for personal value enhancement without the use of force and that affects other individual's ability to achieve their values. Examples include operating a business to provide goods or services to others, smoking in the presence of a non-smoker, driving drunk, teaching physics, etc. Achieving a balance between rights that allow activities that are beneficial or tolerable and prohibiting activities that negatively impact citizens is a major subject of legislation and civil law. The balance is influenced by social norms and conventions or religious beliefs. Wars have been fought over differences of opinion on such subjects. These issues are a major source of disagreement about the proper role of government

Type 3. Acts that result in depriving other individuals of their values through force or the credible threat of force. Examples include rape, robbery, murder, etc. Unless there is extreme stress in a society, most individuals do not engage in these activities. To express this with politically correct words, the "difficult to gratify" engage in these acts, and often end up in prison. "Sensitive" judges often let them out.

The sticky part of segregating type 1 and type 2 efforts is the complex chain of potential cause and effect resulting from a harmless activity. Motorcycle helmet laws provide a good example. The individual motorcyclist may say this is a type 1 activity. He is impacting only himself if he does not wear a helmet. The sponsor of the legislation says the offending cyclist increases the probability that he will become a ward of the state through serious injury. This indirect risk classifies the act as type 2. What does this have to do with designing governments? If a government is to achieve consensus, there must be an appropriate balance between freedom of action and prohibitions that protect individuals. In America today, there is a serious imbalance in prohibiting benign type 2 activities that are purported to create distress to some ill-defined group.

Most citizens would agree that government should not prohibit or interfere with type 1 efforts. Religious associations may disagree and insist that type 1's are grist for the government mill. This point is so fundamental in a liberal society that it is elevated to the first axiom of government.

AXIOM 1—Government will take no actions that interfere with individual efforts that do not cause physical or economic harm to others unless such efforts were a result of prior agreement between the parties involved.

Much interpretation and legal doctrine will evolve around law based on this axiom. The intent is clear. Acts protected by axiom 1 include the withholding of goods or resources owned by the individual. Government cannot force an individual to give owned goods or resources to others because their withholding harms the deprived party. If economic harm done to one individual by another is a result of a prior agreement (contract), then the government must enforce the contract. Incidentally, this axiom eliminates autocratic or dictatorial governments, communism, socialism and welfare states.

Most would agree that government should intervene to prevent type 3 acts. Governments must create "rights" to ensure that individuals cannot deprive others of their values through the use of force or intimidation. This principle is axiom 2:

AXIOM 2—Governments will take the actions necessary to prevent individuals from using force, or the credible threat of force, to harm or achieve efforts not intended or desired by a citizen. The exception to this axiom is the police established by the government. The police may use force or intimidation to achieve behavior compliance.

This axiom is clear and unambiguous. The government will protect individuals from harm caused by others unless police do the harm.

Type 2 efforts are complex only insofar that they must tradeoff one individual's pleasure against another's. This requires delicacy and jurisprudence. When type 2 efforts become the focus of government prohibitions, conflicts result.

Time complicates evaluation of competing values. A resource is worth less in the future than it is now. Economists call this reduction in value with time the discount rate. Since individuals have a finite life, it is more valuable to have goods now than later. How can values be time adjusted when government is investing citizen's money in projects? Should government have a role in imposing a discount rate, particularly when non-renewable resources are involved? From the environmental basket case the USSR left behind, it would appear that the discount rate of politicians and bureaucrats is much higher than capitalists who own the assets they may despoil. The stock market values a security based on the discounted future flow of income that will be generated by the underlying assets, and hence places a significant value on preserving both the productivity and the underlying value of an asset. This valuation prompts the enterprise to avoid despoiling the asset, be it a forest or a factory.

Violent, antisocial behavior must be dealt with in a society where persuasion is the preferred method of achieving compliance with the law. Ultimately, society must use force to constrain or kill some individuals in order to preserve the rights of others. The way government makes these decisions is important and complex. Someone's values will be thwarted. The unwillingness to consider statistical evidence and genetic data is a major problem with the current judicial system. A rational judicial system would consider the cost to society of alternatives and select those that impose the least burden. Frustrated by criminal recidivism, politicians respond by reducing negative law rights of citizens rather that directly attacking the problem of getting the compulsive criminal out of societies way. Compounding this legal myopia is an irrational tendency to support rights created by positive law.

A major flaw in America's judicial system is the principle that judicial decisions should strive to be free of error. This concept supports an archaic jury system that in inefficient and often does not enforce the law. "Beyond reasonable doubt" criteria may be appropriate for cases resulting in severe punishments. A quagmire of technical obstacles prevents the use of statistical or circumstantial evidence. This flaw blocks the prosecution of many violent criminals. At the same time, prosecution for "ideological" crimes, such as drug consumption or prostitution, have swept aside basic constitutional guarantees. It is irrational for a society to attempt to guarantee a "five sigma" guard against wrongful punishment when this process also guarantees near certainty of some recidivist homicidal committing additional murders. The balance between wrongful conviction and the ultimate harm done to new victims is a statistical game that will be played out. The more population densities grow the more imperative that statistical and circumstantial evidence be used to kill or incarcerate violent offenders. The popularity of "three strikes your out" laws reveal the public's position on this matter. Unfortunately this piecemeal approach to the problem will sweep many citizens into the net who are not a threat to society. The perversities of current laws against drug consumption are stuffing the jails with innocent teenagers and forcing the release of criminally insane.

The law in America often declares that withholding an owned resource is equivalent to harming others. This violation of property rights creates endless confusion and conflict in society. When voluntary withholding is illegal, society approaches the anarchy that lack of ownership rules engenders. When the government declares that withholding a resource is a criminal act comparable to type 3 activities, the groundwork is laid for a collapse of ownership rules and hence ultimate anarchy. When a privileged group, selected by the government, is capable of commanding resources they do not own, then communism in its purest form results. The Environmental Protection Agency controls more resources than the largest American corporations.

Several steps in the process of building a good government are accomplished. A precise political vocabulary was defined. The first two (of three) axioms for creating the foundation of the Government were developed. Governments' methods of staffing, selecting functions and methods of organization were described.

The last step in building a science of government is to relate the performance of government to individual's values. This process is imprecise since individuals are not monolithic or consistent in their value structures. Because of various economic interests, different environments and different ideologies, citizens can reflect a kaleidoscope of values. Yet, there is much commonality in the values expressed by individuals. The historical record reveals a diversity of opinion in modern and ancient societies that contain distinct patterns. These patterns are useful in relating governments to values.

CHAPTER 5

▼

MELD AND EGON

"A government big enough to give you everything you want is a government big enough to take from you everything you have."

—Gerald R. Ford

"No one can pretend to love his country and hate his government."

—Bill Clinton

—back to basics

Individuals have a variety of values. Values can focus on consumption, accumulating wealth, or ideology. Some individuals are adamant about the satisfaction of their values; others are less demanding and more flexible in trading the satisfaction of one value for another.

The following pages define several categories of values. Extreme positions taken by individuals are described. New words are introduced to categorizing these "value groupings." The words coined are MELD and EGON. While GLABs may, as individuals, hold Meld or Egon values, as a government employee they become part of the association that supports or thwarts other citizen's values. This chapter explains the complex set of values that define Meld and Egon. The fundamental problem of achieving a broad consensus for government architecture will be reduced to finding values shared by Melds and Egons.

The concept of *Meld* and *Egon* is better understood as an extension of the thoughts of Francis Fukuyama as revealed in his important work *The End of History and the Last Man*. Fukuyama relates all human mental processes to the three elements of *desire*, *reason* and *thymos*. Desire is the process of achieving material and environmental scenarios that provide pleasure. Reason is the tool of natural science, a tool that man has effectively used to achieve his desires and structure his associations. Thymos is the need for recognition. As described by Hegal, man originally distinguished himself from animals by exhibiting a willingness to risk his life in mortal combat in order to satisfy his need for recognition. When some men cowered, the master/slave relationship was born. Modern expressions of thymos are reflected in the striving for political, financial or athletic superiority.

Fukuyama introduces the notion of a directional history by noting that the natural sciences continually build on accumulated knowledge, and hence progresses in a more or less linear manner. Natural science continually increases man's ability to control his environment and escape much of the pain nature can bestow. History has evolved a form of government that best satisfies man's desire and reason; Fukuyama calls this a *liberal democracy*. The progressive collapse of dictatorships and communist governments, and their replacement with liberal democracies is, in Fukuyama's logic, a convincing demonstration of history's direction. Liberal democracies are effective in satisfying desire and reason, but what about thymos? Liberal democracy satisfies man's need for recognition by a mutual recognition of one another, not by the master/slave relationship. This progression may lead to the end of history since there are no further improvements on this final order of liberal democracy, and there are no inherent contradictions in this state of affairs.

As Fukuyama points out, there may be a serious fly in this ointment of liberal democratic contentment. A global mutual admiration society may well not satisfy the thymos of many, or perhaps none of the members of this society. The need of some to achieve recognition by superior performance in business, politics or other endeavors may conflict with the program that aims towards perfectly mutual recognition, particularly if this agenda *imposes* an ultimate egalitarian structure on society. The widespread attempts by Melds to aggressively assure mutual respect by Politically Correct speech codes and the imposition of Herculean efforts to avoid inconveniencing the disabled are only two examples of how the *isothyomatic* fervor can distress the social order. The Egon inherently rejects these notions, insisting that his need for recognition can only be satisfied by an opportunity to excel in some endeavor. As Nietchez laments, such a peaceful and prosperous world of homogenized society leaves "men without chests", and results in a state that is the ultimate disaster rather than "heaven on earth." Thus, rather than being the end of history, the universal adoption of liberal democratic forms of government plants the seeds of its own destruction. In Fukuyama's words: "Is not the *quality* of recognition far more important than its universality? And does not the goal of universalizing recognition inevitably trivialize and de-value it?" As ever-greater government coercion is required to impose a regime of absolute and mutual respect, the Egons rebel and may start the bloody quest for recognition over again. Such a scenario, particularly with nuclear weapons available, is a disturbing thought.

While the advantages of liberal democracy are easy for all to see, there is increasing evidence that the ultimate contradiction is the inability of a liberal democracy to satisfy the citizen's thymos. The primary purpose of this book is to present some fine-tuning on the structure of a liberal democracy, particularly as implemented in America that resolves these contradictions. It may become possible for the lamb to lie down with the lion, but only if the lion has a full belly.

The following questions are polarizing, and intended to reveal the fundamental differences between the Meld and Egon. A brief interpretation of the response expected from each is first provided. Next, quotations from past and present luminaries more eloquently express the position.

While any individual may hold a mixture of Meld and Egon attitudes, it would seem from anecdotal evidence and literature that Meld and Egon are usually found in rather pure form. As the reader proceeds through these 18 questions, he will most likely find his opinions in one or the other camp. If this is true, then the definition of these two categories of human values can lead to a better understanding of our perpetual political conflict.

Human values that reflect man's need for recognition are timeless. It is remarkable that the range of expressed values has remained so consistent over time. Equally evident is the disturbing fact that no society has been structured to accommodate both Meld and Egon. If a government is successful, it must achieve consensus between Meld and Egon. Neither group is likely to go away or significantly change their values. A government design that provides an environment both groups can flourish within is defined in the last chapters of the book. This is the ultimate definition of a "good government", achieving a broad and legitimate consensus among Melds and Egons.

1. What should the government's role be in assuring the proper behavior of individuals?

MELD—The government should take a major and active role in assuring that all individuals behave properly.

> *"if any man after legall conviction shall have or worship any other god, but the lord god, he shall be put to death ..... If any person shall blaspheme the name of god, the father, Sonne or Holie ghost, with direct, expresse, presumptuous or high handed blasphemie, or shall curse God in the like manner, he shall be put to death.",*
> —MASSACHUSSETTS COLONY

EGON—The government's role should be carefully limited. The government can use force only when an individual's behavior is violating the negative law rights of others.

> *"The object of this Essay is to assert one very simple principle,...that the sole end for which mankind are warranted, individually or collectively, in interfering with the liberty of action of any of their number, is self protection. That the only purpose for which power can be rightly exercised over any member of a civilized community, against his will, is to prevent harm to others."*
> —JOHN STUART MILL

2. What is your attitude towards the value of science and reason as a method of directing your efforts? Is the use of intuition, revelation or "faith" superior to reason in such matters?

MELD—My intuition and faith, and innermost feelings of right and wrong are more important and a better guide than science, logic and reason.

> *"We should always be disposed to believe that that which appears to be white is really black, if the hierarchy of the Church so decides."*
>
> —ST. IGNATIUS OF LOYOLA

> *"Anyone therefore who sets out on this field to hunt down final and ultimate truths, truths which are pure or absolutely immutable, will bring home but little, apart from platitudes and commonplaces of the sorriest kind..."*
>
> —FRIEDRICH ENGELS

EGON—I have great confidence in science and reason for the solution of problems and the improvement of my well being than any other body of human knowledge or information, including religion.

> *"I think that in the discussion of natural problems we ought to begin not with the Scriptures, but with experiments and demonstrations."*
>
> —GALILEO GALILEI

"*The great enemy of the truth is very often not the lie—deliberate, contrived, and dishonest—but the myth—persistent, persuasive and realistic. Too often we hold fast to the clichés of our forebears.*"

—JOHN F. KENNEDY

"*Science is the great antidote to the poison of enthusiasm and superstition.*"

—ADAM SMITH

3. Should all laws be applied with consistency? Should exceptions be made to exempt some groups from certain laws because of their social status or position?

MELD—The laws must be applied with consideration for justice and therefore cannot be applied consistently. Congress must be exempt in order to act decisively. Affirmative action is just since in compensates for past wrongs.

> *"When a president does it then it is not illegal."*
> —RICHARD M. NIXON

> *"Forget about civil rights. I'm talking about Black Power."*
> —FLOYD BIXLER McKISSICK.

EGON—The greatest value of law is its impartiality and consistency. Once a single judge's opinion of justice intervenes in the application of the law, the law is reduced to rule by man.

> *"No freeman shall be taken, or imprisoned, or outlawed, or exiled, or in any way harmed, nor will we go upon him, nor will we send upon him, except by the legal judgment of his peers, or by the law of the land."*
> —MAGNA CARTA

"*The Constitution of the United States is a law for rulers and people, equally in war and peace, and covers with the shield of its protection all classes of men, at all times, and under all circumstances. No doctrine involving more pernicious consequences was ever invented by the wit of man than that any of its provisions can be suspended during any of the great exigencies of government. Such a doctrine leads directly to anarchy or despotism...*"

—DAVID DAVIS

"*For de little stealin' dey gits you in jail soon or late. For the big stealin' dey makes you emperor and puts you in de Hall o' Fame when you croaks.*"

—EUGENE O'NEILL

4. Is altruism good or bad?

MELD—The act of helping others, even to the point of sacrifice for self and family is an ultimate good and is an important part of the success and value of human society.

> *"A man is truly ethical only when he obeys the compulsion to help all life which he is able to assist, and shrinks from injuring anything that lives."*
>
> —ALBERT SCHWEITZER"

> *"The man who lives for self alone*
> *Lives for the meanest mortal known.*
>
> —JOAQUIN MILLER

EGON Altruism is bad in every respect; it weakens the giver and the recipient. Social order must be based on respect for social conventions and law. Enlightened self-interest generates the most successful and happiest societies.

> *"Charity is twice cursed—it hardens him that gives and softens him that takes."*
>
> —BOUCK WHITE

> *"A race of altruists is necessarily a race of slaves. A race of free men is necessarily a race of egoists.*
>
> —MAX STIRNER

"*To command to love our neighbors as ourselves…is impossible to fulfill; such an enormous inflation of love can only lower its value and not remedy the evil. Civilization pays no heed to all this.*"

—SIGMUND FREUD

5. Is capitalism and the accumulation of wealth good or bad for a society

MELD—Capitalism is bad, it brings out the most evil and disgusting traits in people, such as the accumulation of wealth. Society should minimize capitalism's influence through government control.

> *"Capitalism…is not intelligent, it is not beautiful, it is not just, it is not virtuous—and it doesn't deliver the goods."*
> —JOHN MAYNARD KEYNES

> *"Socialism is the abolition of human self-alienation, the return of man as a real human being."*
> —ERICH FROMM

EGON Capitalism is good for society and the individual. Economic freedom is the foundation of all other freedoms and of human happiness.

> *"Private property was the original source of freedom. It is still is its main bulwark."*
> —WALTER LIPPMANN

> *"Private Property, the Law of Accumulation of Wealth, and the Law of Competition…these are the highest results of human experience, the soil in which society so far has produced the best fruit."*
> —ANDREW CARNEGIE

"The inherent vice of Capitalism is the unequal sharing of blessings; the inherent vice of Socialism is the equal sharing of miseries."

—WINSTON CHURCHILL

6. What is your attitude towards human beings; are they intrinsically good or bad; are the human race's accomplishments to be admired or despised?

MELD—Human beings have many bad and disgusting qualities, such as greed and aggressiveness. Some are exemplary good but most of the human race is disgusting and overpopulating the earth.

> *"Man is nothing else than fetid sperm, a sack of dung, the food for worms…You have never seen a viler dunghill."*
> —ST. BERNARD OF CLAIRVAUX

> *"Perhaps the only true dignity of man is his capacity to despise himself."*
> —GEORGE SANTAYANA

> *"The white race is the cancer of history. It is the white race and it alone—its ideologies and inventions—which eradicates autonomous civilizations wherever it spreads……"*
> —SUSAN SONTAG

EGON The human race is admirable and elegant, and their achievements are marvels of beauty and strength. The continued application of science and technology with the introduction of sensible governments will allow the earth's population to stabilize and achieve ever-higher quality of life.

> *"My aim is the re-establishment of the worship of man."*
> —GABRIELE D'ANNUNZIO

"Give me your tired, your poor.
Your huddled masses yearning to breathe free,
The wretched refuse of your teeming shore,
Send these, the homeless, tempest-tossed to me,
I lift my lamp beside the golden door!

—EMMA LAZARUS

7. Is your personal judgment on moral and political issues superior and more correct than others, even if the other opinions are rendered by trustworthy people who have though about the issues more deeply?

MELD I know what is right and wrong although others appear to be confused. I know I am right about the issues of religion, altruism and moral behavior.

> *"Burn the libraries, for their value is in this one book (the Koran)."*
>
> —OMAR I

> *"When the consensus of scholarship says one thing and the Word of God another, the consensus of scholarship can go plumb to hell for all I care.*
>
> —WILLIAM A. SUNDAY

EGON—I acknowledge and respect alternative moral and social systems; I do not claim superiority for preferred values. However, if an alternative ideology insists on establishing itself at the exclusion of others, thereby denying individual rights, it should be destroyed or rendered impotent.

> *"Nothing in the world is more dangerous than a sincere ignorance and conscientious stupidity."*
>
> —MARTIN LUTHER KING, JR

"*It is forbidden to decry other sects; the true believer gives honor to whatever in them is worthy of honor.*"

—ASOKA

"*Those who are convinced they have a monopoly on The Truth always feel that they are only saving the world when they slaughter the heretics.*"

—ARTHUR M. SCHLESINGER

8. Is it good or bad to have an unequal distribution of wealth? If bad, who should oversee the redistribution?

MELD It is basically wrong to have extreme disparity in wealth, either within our country or in the world. Only a powerful central authority can overcome the greed of individuals and assure an egalitarian outcome.

> *"As political equality is the remedy for political tyranny, so is economic equality the only way of putting an end to the economic tyranny exercised by the few over the many through the superiority of wealth."*
>
> —EDWARD BELLAMY

> *"The law, in its majestic equality, forbids the rich as well as the poor to sleep under bridges, to beg in the streets, and to steal bread."*
>
> —ANATOLE FRANCE

EGON—There is nothing morally wrong with uneven distribution of wealth, and in a capitalist society, it provides the incentives for production that benefits all. Government seizure of one individuals wealth, without their consent and for whatever purpose is by far the greater evil and is socially destructive.

> *"We are in danger of developing a cult of the Common Man, which means a cult of mediocrity.*
>
> —HERBERT CLARK HOOVER

"*Equality I spoke the word As if a wedding vow Ah, but I was so much older then I'm younger than that now.*"

—BOB DYLAN

"*Every individual endeavors to employ his capital so that its produce may be of greatest value...He intends only his own security, only his own gain...By pursuing his own interest he frequently promotes that of society more effectively than when he really intends to promote it.*"

—ADAM SMITH

9. Is the conduct of war an acceptable and honorable activity for a government to engage in? Should one or a few leaders be able to initiate war?

MELD I believe in pacifism and reject the concept of war as immoral and unjustified under any circumstances.

> *"Man has no right to kill his brother. It is no excuse that he does so in uniform: he only adds the infamy of servitude to the crime of murder."*
> —PERCY BYSSHE SHELLEY

> *"Military service produces moral imbecility, ferocity and cowardice."*
> —BERNARD SHAW.

EGON I respects the warrior and acknowledges warfare as an essential part of the social order. I do not want leaders to engage in fruitless or stupid wars, but I support warfare as the last alternative for defending the nation or preserving important values. I also prefer an all-volunteer militia.

> *"No triumph of peace is so great as the supreme triumph of war."*
> —THEODORE ROOSEVELT

"Eternal peace is a dream, and not even a beautiful one, and war is a part of God's world order. In it are developed the noblest virtues of man, courage and abnegation, dutifulness and self-sacrifice at the risk of life. Without war the world would sink to materialism."

—HELMUTH VON MOLTKE

10. Do you feel that every individual should be free to express, either through words, art or music, any concept, thought or interpretation they choose?

MELD—Certain social and group values are more important than freedom of expression. Anyone who denounces my dogma, or expresses what I feel is patently offensive, should not be allowed to do so under the threat of government force. Only a government can stop the expression of such bad ideas.

> *"It is the absolute right of the State to supervise the formation of public opinion"*
>
> —PAUL JOSEPH GOEBBELS

> *"The liberty of thinking and publishing whatsoever each one likes, without any hindrances, is not in itself an advantage over which society can wisely rejoice. On the contrary, it is the fountainhead and origin of many evils."*
>
> —LEO XIII

EGON—Freedom of expression is essential, fundamental and of critical importance to me as an individual and to the welfare of society. Just as economic freedom is essential to a healthy economy, freedom of expression is the cornerstone of a market of ideas. No one has a monopoly on "correct" ideas.

> *"The essence of the free press is the reliable, reasonable and moral nature of freedom. The character of the censored press is the nondescript confusion of tyranny."*
>
> —KARL MARX

"*Freedom of expression is the well-spring of our civilization… The history of civilizations in considerable measure the displacement of error which once held sway as official truth by beliefs which in turn have yielded to other truths. Therefore the liberty of man to search for truth ought not to be fettered, no matter what orthodoxy's he may challenge. Liberty of thought soon shrivels without freedom of expression. Nor can truth be pursued in an atmosphere hostile to the endeavor or under dangers which are hazarded only by heroes.*"

—FELIX FRANKFURTER

11. Do you feel that you are more important as a member of a group than as an individual and member of a family? Do you feel best when commended by a large group (who you may not know individually), or when recognized and accepted by your family or a small group of associates who you know and respect?

MELD—My life is most fulfilled when a large group who I may not know as individuals recognizes me. My church, my political precinct, the group at my club or my gang is significant. I would like to be recognized by the world as an important person.

> *"Individual liberty, freed from all bonds and all laws, all objective and social values, is in reality only a death dealing anarchy."*
> —PIUS XII

> *"Mankind's salvation lies exclusively in everyone's making everything his business, in the people of the East being anything but indifferent to what is thought in the West, and in the people of the West being anything but indifferent to what happens in the East. Literature, one of the most sensitive and responsible tools of human existence, has been the first to pick up, adopt, and assimilate this sense of the growing unity of mankind."*
> —ALEXANDER I. SOLZHENITSYN

EGON—The most important recognition is that of my family; and myself only when I feel that I have made an accomplishment will the recognition of others be meaningful. I am most pleased by recognition of a few colleagues who I know well and respect; the adoration of a large crowd is meaningless.

"This Nobel precept is often cited by Plato: "Do thine own work, and know thyself." Each of these two parts generally cover the whole duty of man, and each includes the other. He who will do his own work well, discovers that his first lesson is to know himself, and what is his duty."
—MICHEL YQUEM DEMONTAIGNE

12. Do you believe that when you are engaged in advocacy that telling the truth is more important than achieving your advocacy goals? Do the ends justify the means?

MELD Telling a lie for a worthy cause is fully justified. Besides, the truth is always relative. No one can say that a lie is absolute. Worthy causes are more important than processes.

> *"When the end is lawful, the means are also lawful."*
> —HERMANN BUSENBAUM

> *"History will absolve me."*
> —FIDEL CASTRO

EGON—Objective, scientific truth is the cornerstone of civilized society, and is the most important principle and cause. Any cause that requires a lie to succeed deserves to die. Telling a public lie is the most anti-social act one can commit.

> *"Seek the truth*
> *Listen to the truth*
> *Teach the truth*
> *Love the truth*
> *Abide by the truth*
> *And defend the truth*
> *Unto death."*
>
> —JOHN HUS

> *"Our belief in truth itself, that there is a truth, and that our minds and it are made for each other,—what is it but a passionate affirmation of desire, in which our social system backs us up?"*
> —WILLIAM JAMES

13. Are genes important in determining human behavior? Is the behavior of humans more influenced by genetics or by the conditioning of parents and society?

MELDS—The dominant factor in determining behavior is the environment around the child and young adult. The mental processes (ignoring the known heritable physical disorders) are molded primarily by the environment; physical, emotional and intellectual.

> *"Evil is not inherent in nature, it is learned."*
> —ASHLEY MONTAGUE

EGON—Significant personality traits, particularly those leading to excessive violence and anti-social behavior are heritable. While we do not fully understand the consequences of heredity, based on pragmatic observations of families and friends, there is strong correlation's between social behavior and genes. Science will continue to reveal the truth of this matter, and we are ready to accept the facts regardless of their outcomes.

> *"It is better for all the world, if instead of waiting to execute degenerate offspring for crime, or let them starve for their imbecility, society can prevent those who are manifestly unfit from continuing their kind. The principle that sustains compulsory vaccination is broad enough to cover cutting the Fallopian tubes... Three generations of imbeciles are enough."*
> —OLIVER WENDELL HOLMES

14 When an individual commits a violent anti-social act, depriving others of their basic rights to life, liberty and the pursuit of happiness, should that individual be held responsible and pay the designated penalty, or should society shoulder part or all of the blame.

MELD—The dominant factor in creating the mental processes that led to the destructive action was caused by an inadequate environment, and society is largely responsible for failing to provide that environment.

> *"Man is not born wicked; he becomes so in the same way he becomes sick."*
>
> —VOLTAIRE

> *"Remember particularly that you cannot be a judge of anyone. For no one can judge a criminal, until he recognizes that he is just such a criminal as the man standing before him, and that he perhaps is more than all men to blame for the crime. When he understands that, he will be able to be a judge."*
>
> —FYODOR DOSTOYEVSKI.

EGON—Each individual has control of his own mind and is responsible for his own behavior. If he is mentally ill he should be locked up out of harms way. If he insists on committing anti-social acts and exhibits normal mental responses, then death or imprisonment is the only alternative.

> *"the ideal of a government of laws and not of men is all that stands between a free society and totalitarianism."*
>
> —F. A. HAYEK

15. Most individuals have a set of values that expresses a preference for social structures, constitutions, laws, etc. Do you believe that your justification for these values is based on abstract concepts of "what should be", or are they based on pragmatic observations of the real world.

MELD Values are not relative; they are absolute. I know what is right and wrong, and the way society should be is according to these rules. Human beings are often bad, and trying to order society to accommodate their perversity is wrong.

> *"For Truth is the Unity of the universal and subjective Will; and the Universal is to be found in the State, its laws, its universal and rational arrangements. The State is the Divine Idea as it exists on Earth."*
> —GEORG WILHELM FRIEDRICH HEGEL

EGON—That social order that best accommodates human nature will succeed. The basic self-centeredness and concern about self and family first is both honest and provides a solid foundation for a stable and productive society.

> *"It is doubtful if the oppressed ever fight for freedom. They fight for pride and for power to oppress others. The oppressed want above all to imitate their oppressors; they want to retaliate."*
> —ERIC HOFFER

"*People fight for luxuries, for power, or for ideas with just as much passion as they fight for money. Interests may be reconciled, but not philosophies… The desire for power is no less basic than the desire for wealth.*"

—ASOKA

16. The earth's environment has become a subject of debate. What balance should be achieved between human needs and preserving the environment?

MELD The long-term health of the planet is more important than human beings. Industrialization should be stopped and everyone impoverished to the point of reducing the population in order to avoid the apocalypse that will befall us if we continue increasing population and wealth.

> *"Most convincing as evidence of populousness, we men have actually become a burden to the earth, the fruits of nature hardly suffice to sustain us, there is a general pressure of scarcity giving rise to complaints, since the earth can no longer support us."*
> —TERTULLIAN (AD 200)

EGON Modern technology is perfectly capable of correcting environmental damage while continuing to support a much larger population with ever increasing wealth. Human existence and happiness is the most important consideration. All objective evidence denies the predictions of doom that will be caused by growing populations and wealth.

> *"After the balloon bursts on global warming and it has been incorporated like overpopulation, resource depletion, biotech plagues, and the ozone hole into the conventional wisdom of doom, to what new doom will the environmentalist millenarians turn next? What new crises can be conjured up and used to promote their sociopolitical engineering schemes while enhancing their power and influence over the worlds governments?"*
> —RONALD BAILEY

17. Try to project the future of the human race several hundred years from now. Is the situation at that time likely to be an improvement on the current state of affairs, or is it likely to be worse

MELD The world at that time is likely to be a miserable place. There will be overpopulation, increasing pollution, depletion of resources and famines.

> *"The beginning of the end"*
> —PAUL EHRLICH

EGON The rapid pace of improvements in agriculture, manufacturing, materials and data processing will allow the continuation of a long trend which has increased food and wealth faster than population growth. The poorer nations can achieve greater wealth while reducing pollution.

> *"Taking a very gloomy view of the future of the human race, let us suppose that it can only expect to survive for two thousand million years longer, a period about equal to the past age of the earth."*
> —SIR JAMES HOPWOOD JEANS

18. Should individuals be allowed to possess arms? Does the Constitutional right to bear arms include individual's possession of deadly weapons?

MELD The vague wording of the constitution does not justify the dangers to society which possession of firearms creates. Only the police and the government militia should be allowed to possess dangerous weapons.

"Political power grows out of the barrel of a gun."
—**MAO TSE-TUNG**

"I propose getting rid of conventional armaments and replacing them with reasonably priced hydrogen bombs that would be distributed equally throughout the world."
—**IDI AMIN**

EGON An armed citizenry is the ultimate guarantee against the government usurping power and authority over the individual. Training and prohibitions against criminal use of guns will diminish the dangers. The loss of a few lives each year due to accidents or criminal use of firearms does not justify rendering civil society defenseless against criminals and governments.

"The people who are pushing gun control know it won't affect professional criminals, but they can't effectively counter this argument because the criminals they're worried about are us, you and me......... They are afraid of us."
—**KEN GRISSOM, The Huston Post**

CHAPTER 6

▼

THE GOOD, THE
BAD AND THE UGLY

"I would that the last king were strangled with the guts of the last priest"

—Jean Meslier

—more evil or less good?

Governments have wreaked various forms of havoc on their citizens. Some have been brutal and destructive beyond comprehension. The Khmer Rouge in Cambodia provides a timeless example of the Ugly. Some governments have redistributed wealth to the point of transforming their safety nets into dependency traps. These "welfare states" bankrupt the economy while destroying incentives for enterprise. Such well-intentioned efforts are bad, not ugly. A few governments are good; they allow citizens to achieve their values.

The advocates of a particular form of government define "goodness" in terms of how well a government fits the image of the advocates' ideology. A despot will financially rape his nation to aggrandize himself and a loyal band of tyrants. Their definition of "good" is different from the citizens. Allowing the government to define the criteria for success is putting the fox in charge of the chicken coop. If a government is to achieve consensus, the evaluation of government must be in the hands of those citizens *whose livelihood does not depend upon* government's *wealth redistribution.*

Debate about government leads to barroom brawls and wars. Most treatises that espouse the virtues of a particular type of government end up "preaching to the choir." The only events that change citizens' minds are changes in economic circumstances or other personal discomforts. Ideology often contradicts reason. The Cuban revolutionaries are a stark example.

Many criteria have been proposed to measure social good. From Hume's calculus of the greatest good for the greatest number, to Hitlerian definitions which prize survivability and racial purity. Academics and politicians insist on defining what is good for their fellow citizens. These measures seldom relate to citizens' values.

No government can please all of the people all of the time. Governments usually displease most people all of the time. The republican form of government places dangerous powers in the hands of unscrupulous people, allowing them to plunder and rape the economy. Autocracies attract mad megalomaniacs as leaders and destroy wealth and freedom. Attempts at achieving communism or democracy have always degenerated into either an autocracy or a republic. These forms of government have demonstrated their inability to create a society of *consensus* and *creation.* If legitimacy and consensus is the goal, government must limit what it tries to do. This is not all bad.

The ultimate measure of a government's performance is how fully the citizens can fulfill their values. This is different from the utilitarian and socialist measure that demands the greatest benefit for the greatest number. The socialist measure of benefit presumes a person or group, always in the government's employee, will measure the sum of benefits. This leads to the same tyrannies as any autocracy, regardless of the egalitarian proclamations made by the government. If the measure of value is left to the individual, this dilemma disappears. The government should not be concerned by how an individual spends his time or resources as long as these activities do not diminish the values of his fellow citizens.

Many melds have problems with a measure of government performance chosen by the citizens. They are convinced that some citizens have values that are not in their own best interests. These Melds are the ones who want to legislate personal behavior and create "first person" or "victimless" crimes. This attitude reveals the most fundamental difference between Meld and Egon. A current example of this dichotomy is the conflicts generated over environmental salvation. Science has discovered many environmental problems created by industrialization. Progress has been made in finding solutions. Effective solutions are being implemented, but often require a compromise between industrial efficiency and the environment. The collectivists have seized on this issue as a mechanism for convincing individuals that they will perish unless the Melds take over government. The last Meld bandwagon was central economic planning versus free markets. That one did not work out well either. The citizens must be on guard against infection by the collectivist germs hidden in the appealing fruit of environmental salvation. It is hardly a coincidence that Michael Gorbachev, one of the worlds most prominent, outspoken and consistent collectivist, has established his world wide advocacy efforts as an environmental crusade, the Green Cross

—what citizens want

The best governments allow citizen's to achieve their values. A government designer must know how citizens judge government. These measures are:

WEALTH Per-capita wealth and the rate of growth is an important measure. If the nation has a convertible currency, wealth per capita is easily measured. The distribution of wealth is important for achieving growth. Highly skewed distributions or flat ones indicate poor government performance. Melds advocate egalitarian distributions. When governments try to force egalitarian distributions, the result is usually a more skewed distribution than in free market economies. More wealth is always better. Luddites are free to deny themselves of wealth so produced. The preferred distribution is normal, not uniform or highly skewed. While some perverted citizens may relish the fact that no one is wealthier than they, most sensible people simply want *more*.

HEALTH Life expectancy, distribution of age at death, and incidence of disease and incapacitation are important determinants of well-being. Rates of hospitalization and waiting times for serious medical procedures are important to citizen's values. Governments affect health in a variety of ways, most often by creating constraints that are detrimental to health care providing enterprises. The health measure must include injuries caused by malicious acts of societies' members and accidents. Some damage from violence is the inevitable price society pays for individual rights and growth in wealth. Inept governments severely exacerbate these problems. Governments can minimize injuries from accidents or criminal acts by a judicious blending of negative law rights and positive law constraints on behavior.

NATIONAL SURVIVAL Since the dawn of time, any tribe or nation, no matter how bucolic, has been susceptible to plunder and annihilation by warlike neighbors. A prerequisite for enjoying wealth and health is integrity of the nation and the social order. The need for protection is infrequently exercised. The stronger the defenses, the less likely they are to be tested. Having an effective defense when needed is imperative. A government caught with its powder wet when challenged by a well-armed aggressor can quickly dissipate any other benefits. For those who believe the world has outgrown such nonsense, take a closer look at North Korea, Iran and Iraq. Societies are well advised to err in the direction of excess when preparing defenses.

FAIRNESS When governments exercise force, citizens expect fair treatment. If privileged classes or government staff is not subject to the same enforcement of positive law, or negative law does not equally protect some, then the government is inconsistent. In this context, "fair" does not have moral or ethical implications. Fairness is consistent application of all law, both positive and negative. Issues of welfare are separate from fairness and consistency. Laws resulting in redistribution that are motivated by altruism, pity, preventing anti-social disruption, or greed can not be confused with "fairness." Fairness is the consistent application of law. Any law, such as "affirmative action", that selectively applies constraints or benefits is in total contradiction of this principle.

EFFICIENCY When governments perform functions that benefit citizens, it is important that these functions be accomplished efficiently. If the government consumes excessive resources in its efforts, then fewer resources are available to satisfy citizens' values. The percentage of gross domestic product consumed by the government is a superficial measure. Some positive law can affect both GDP and the share that government consumes. Governments may decide to accept enormous inefficiency's in the redistribution of goods to maintain control of their citizens. The citizens are often duped into believing that government is the source of all wealth.

Produced wealth that is diverted to projects of the government's choice does little to satisfy citizen's values. The construction of a super-conducting super-collider or a space station, no matter how efficient, could hardly satisfy the values of more than a handful of citizens. Citizens may be temporarily diverted by appeals to preserve the society or accomplish great feats (like landing a person on the moon). Continued sacrifice for unnecessary government projects wears thin, even when advocated by the most eloquent demagogues.

ENVIRONMENT Government can contribute to or allow others to create environmental hazards. Environmental hazards can have a negative impact on health, wealth and values. The shocking disregard of the USSR for polluting industries should put to rest the illusion that governments are natural protectors of the environment. Resources directed to environmental protection are consumed to provide future benefits. The proper discount rate for society's investment in the future of the "commons" is a legitimate role for government. This role cannot be perverted by MELDS to create an overriding government presence, as is happening in America and Europe today. As Murray Bookchin confesses "I believe that the color of radicalism today is not red, but green." When some associations can effectively externalize the real cost of production by polluting, it is reasonable for government to force internalization of these costs. Removing the hazard or paying the affected party's compensation can accomplish this. Environmental concerns have presented Melds an opportunity to embrace environmental causes as the reason politicians should be in charge of an authoritarian government. These arguments are even more specious than those based on economics and social welfare.

INFRASTRUCTURE is like other goods and services except it can infringe property rights. Roads, telephone and power wires, gas and water lines must be built to support all households and businesses in a region. There is a fuzzy line between infrastructure built by governments and the private sector. The private sector is more efficient. Projects like highways or power distribution lines may be difficult to achieve without government intervention. This intervention can be through eminent domain taking of land and/or constructing the projects. Infrastructure is important for generating wealth and health. Infrastructure for transportation and communications nurtures many rights. The use of inside information prior to the exercise of eminent domain has provided a source of extra-curricular wealth for politicians. Glabs often overbuild infrastructure in order to garner the gifts of construction and real estate interests.

CONFLICT can occur as internal strife within an association or through international challenges to national sovereignty. The frequency and intensity of conflict are an important measure of a government's performance. Some conflicts are created by mean-spirited neighboring nations or crazy homicidal citizens (those with difficult to gratify values). Some governments have a propensity to precipitate conflicts unnecessarily. A good government should minimize domestic and international conflicts without sacrificing other performance measures. When international conflicts do arise, it is imperative that government is capable of mounting adequate defenses.

INCARCERATION The number of citizens deprived of their values by incarceration is a measure of government performance. If a government can lay claim to a consensus of its citizens, then it should not have to put too many in jail. There will always be some mentally ill or alienated individuals who are violent and prone to commit type 3 acts. These individuals must be isolated from society, killed or modified. Cruel and unusual punishments should be judged in the context of the misery caused by the perpetrator to other citizens. The tendency of coercive central governments to put a large fraction of their citizens in jail is evident in America. The percent of citizens in prison has tripled in twenty years. The number of American citizens in jail on drug consumption charges and other "first person" crimes is an indictment of the legislature. Several federal judges have resigned or refused to hear drug cases because of the perversity of severe mandatory sentences for an act that should be legal in the first place. The legislation that allows law enforcement officials to seize property without due process is an extension of this travesty. The argument that these personal consumption preferences will lead to other destructive acts is specious. There are adequate laws against destructive acts. The underground market for a popular but illegal recreation causes "Drug violence." A corollary of the over zealous incarceration of teen-age marijuana smokers is the release of criminally insane murderers and rapists. American governments have forgotten the experience with prohibiting ethanol consumption.

RIGHTS are valued by most citizens. Rights must be aggressively safeguarded by the judicial and police. These safeguards are important ideological and practicable performance parameters for a government. Negative law rights are more uniformly valued but positive law rights are often important for the designated recipients of the redistributed resources. As with other laws, consistent enforcement of rights better satisfies citizen's values.

VISION Governments may or may not offer visions. It is not necessary, but it's a nice touch; especially if the visions are pleasant ones. "A chicken in every pot" is certainly better than "blood, sweat and tears." Nations are not always in control of their visions. It is better to have a nice vision than an ugly one. The vision of an ever-expanding government is not pleasant for most citizens. Reality supports a pleasant vision of the future if governments stop interfering. Effective government can allow the citizens to create greater wealth, minimize poverty and maximize freedom from conflict.

▼

CHAPTER 7

FUTURES

"Necessity is the plea of every infringement of human freedom. It is the argument of tyrants; it is the creed of slaves."

—William Pitt

—seeing clearly now

Science predicts what will happen when physical parameters are known or controlled. Before reason and science, the shaman or priest claimed to own all predictive powers. These mystics guarded their methodology carefully. Science uses logic and experiment to predict outcomes. The data and reasoning is exposed so it can be reproduced and verified by others. The scientific method is anathema to shamans, priests and congressmen.

Science uses naturally occurring or man made scenarios to predict outcomes. An astronomer will observe the position and state of stars and planets to predict future positions. Engineers use science to control relevant variables so the future can be predicted and managed in a manner pleasing to the designer. The results of engineering, from large buildings, highways and B-747s, do not necessarily please all individuals all of the time. So it is bound to be with political engineering. The science of government is no exception to these principles. There are many variables that the government designer can control. As the numbers of variables becomes large, it is difficult to predict how a government architecture will work. The more functions a government elects to perform and the more complex their organizations, the more difficult to predict the outcome. Buildings should not fall down in a windstorm and B-747s should not crash when landing. Governments should meet similar expectations of performance. They do not. If the average glab had to meet the professional standards of competence and honesty of an architect or engineer, many of society's problems would have been resolved.

A science of government can allow citizens to realize their values. The designer tries for perfection. There will always be a few citizens that are unhappy unless the government caters to their particular ideology or greed. The most perturbing examples are those who become upset with fellow citizens who are happy. These "difficult to gratify" may be impossible to bring into a consensus. If their disaffection persists they become the antisocial and violent members of society. Government can exacerbate this problem by raising false expectations of the less endowed citizens in return for votes. Higher population densities require that society become less tolerant of anti-social behavior. Teen-age males are like molecules of a gas; the more they are compressed the hotter they get, exploding if constrained. The most sincere counseling is not likely to change millennia of evolution that has produced the wiring diagram of a teen-age gang member; particularly when the opportunity to socialize him early in life was lost. If the thin veneer of civility is omitted or delaminated by a child's environment, the result is a savage and unreasoning beast.

When designing a building, the soil conditions, climatic and geological environments must be defined before the foundation, structural and climate control systems can be designed. So it is with the government designer. The scenario of demographics, resource availability and the citizen's values must be defined first. An engineer applies the knowledge of materials and physical laws to his project. The competent design of a government requires no less. The distribution and characteristics of individuals is as important as the environment and resources available.

The next step is to describe the scenarios that will prevail in America. These scenarios will provide the foundation for the Government architecture. Some of these scenarios are certain to evolve, barring global catastrophes such as nuclear war or asteroid impact. Other variables can be determined by the government, and are subject to a "feedback" effect. Often the complex interactions of the social order result in government actions producing events other than intended. Good engineers should always take into account these "second order" effects when designing a system.

Twelve irreversible trends are:

1. Communications will be more efficient, more available and cost less. Satellite, wireless and fiber optic technology provide access to broadcast data, database access by individuals and one-one communications. This trend will prevent governments from denying citizens information. The liberalization of the USSR and China was hastened by information technology. Other authoritarian governments will be equally frustrated. Combined with more powerful data processing, the communications trend will profoundly change the delivery of education, information and entertainment services.

2. There will be more people on earth. Regardless of the immigration barriers erected, the races of European origin will become a smaller fraction of the population; even in North America and Europe. Asian populations will increase in absolute and relative terms. World population will grow to 10–12 billion before sufficient wealth is generated to slow birth rates to equilibrium. Contrary to popular hysteria, there will

be no overall food shortages or environmental catastrophes while this growth occurs. The world rate of reproduction has fallen from 4.2 in 1975 to 3.3 in 1991. A value of 2.1 yields approximate population stability. Population stability could be achieved in the first half of this century without extreme measures advocated by deep greens. Most indigenous European populations are reproducing at less than the equilibrium rate. Good governments that create wealth and make modern birth control technology available can accelerate the trend towards population stability. The ugly governments in Africa, as a counterexample of the sensible, have kept that resource rich country in poverty for decades. The companion of poverty is high birth rates.

3. The trend towards free trade is irreversible and will result in more equalization of wealth throughout the world. The trade barriers that rich countries have erected against the poor have caused more unnecessary poverty than the ill-advised efforts of the World Bank, IMF and foreign aid have alleviated. Even the vile governments in Vietnam, North Korea and Cuba will participate in trade as their senile governments die. As the "third world" countries wealth grows with decreasing trade barriers and better governments, their population growth will slow. The trend towards a global economy will result in greater equalization of wealth, possibly with a temporary decline in absolute per capita wealth in the rich countries. This result was promised but never achieved by all the egalitarian governments in the world. Global output of goods will increase. These trends will stress the patience of the wealthy democracies for free trade. As flexible, automated manufacturing technology matures, more effort will be focused on services and knowledge work. There will be less reason to incur the transportation costs of moving goods. Computer-controlled robots will produce goods. The information required to program the robot is more easily transported than the items produced. The importance of trade in manufactured goods will diminish. The movement of information and knowledge will become global. Intellectual property protection becomes more significant.

4. Defensive weapons will become more effective and cheaper. This nullifies the historical leverage of offensive weapons. A missile that has a high probability of killing a main battle tank or an attack aircraft will cost much less than the attacking platform and requires one soldier to operate. The tank or aircraft costs millions of dollars and requires dozens of support and operational personnel. The use of Stinger surface-to-air missiles in Afghanistan cost the USSR many helicopters and fixed wing aircraft. The cost of the Stingers was insignificant. Commercial technologies available to third world countries can be used to build effective defensive weapons. The economics of conquest become less attractive. This trend will be paralleled by proliferation of nuclear and biological weapons of primitive but effective varieties. These "weapons of mass destruction" are best suited to national blackmail by rouge governments or by ideological terrorists. Weapons of mass destruction are of little use in subjugating nations; this requires a bayonet under each chin. The Global Positioning System's precise navigation capability makes conventional high explosive warheads accurate to within a few feet of the target. Precision weapon delivery can nullifying rouge regimes that use sophisticated tunneling to protect their weapon complexes and general staff. New "brilliant" weapons provide super accurate delivery. This capability adds little to offensive strikes intended to subjugate populations, but precision weapons can be used for surgical strikes to take out biological weapons factories, command and control centers and other targets critical to a terrorist nation.

5. The health of citizens will benefit from data processing, communications and medical technology. The application of new technologies to medicine will improve effectiveness, consistency of treatment and reduce cost. This trend will result in better and cheaper drugs, accurate and inexpensive automated diagnostics and automated surgical procedures. This trend is slowed, but not crippled by the objections of adamant medical practitioners' unions and the introduction of nationalized health care schemes. Genetic sciences will progress in spite of the efforts of Jeremy Rifkin and his brownshirts. A major unknown

is what society will choose to do with this knowledge. Genetic science will predict the probability of an individual contracting a heritable disease. This makes statistical underwriting of health or life insurance difficult. Insurance companies will refuse to write policies for those prone to early disease or death. Society will have to choose between allowing individuals with inherited disorders to go untreated; or providing treatment through a government funded or mandated health care scheme. If the latter, the government will control triage. The potential for genetic sciences to cure heritable disease is not yet proven, but likely to emerge from future research. The trends in medical sciences will shift the age distribution toward the elderly and reduce birth rates in concert with rising wealth. The potential for "fixing" mental disorder by genetic manipulation makes the prospect of a government controlled health care system more frightening than the economic disaster it would wreak.

6. The fraction of wealth devoted to environmental remediation will increase. Wealthy nations will step up to this challenge faster than poor ones. Elected governments will respond to environmental needs. Russia provides an example of how bad environmental neglect can get. Greens argue that the discount rate private capital applies to investments rule out significant environmental improvements and resource conservation without government coercion. The record of the USSR and the US Interior Department would indicate the opposite is true. Glabs have higher discount rates, usually dictated by the next crises they create. As populations grow and become wealthier, a greater fraction of GDP will be devoted to environmental improvement. This will occur fastest in the wealthier countries. This trend will tend to equalize *consumable* per capita wealth between the richer and poorer countries.

7. No serious commodity shortages will occur barring global catastrophes such as asteroid impact or nuclear war. A combination of conservation and substitution of more abundant resources for scarcer ones will be driven by market forces. Examples include the substitution of

sand (fiber optic cables) for copper in "wired" communications and the substitution of dirt (ceramics and carbon composites) for metals. Increasing productivity of agricultural and mineral recovery processes will ensure an abundance of food and raw materials. Conservation and recycling will solve water and energy resource problems. All of these trends were established long ago. The availability of commodity and food resources continues to outpace the growth in population. These trends will continue to disappoint the post-Malthus malthusians.

8. Manufacturing processes will become more efficient and flexible. Improvements in automation and process control require less input of material and labor per unit of output. New materials, such as carbon composites and ceramics consume only renewable resources and energy. Recycling of metals and plastics is becoming economical. Some European countries and American communities, caught up in the ecological frenzy, have legislated recycling beyond any economic benefits. This imposes unjustified costs on their citizens. As non-renewable fossil fuel supplies dwindle in a few hundred years, fusion, solar and fission power sources will be developed. France and Japan are primarily dependent upon nuclear fission for electrical supplies. New fuel cycles for exotic batteries will allow the continued evolution of personal transportation with diversity of destinations. Demand for heavy materials used in housing and transportation will decline as populations stabilize and the materials become more durable or recyclable.

9. Data processing power will continue to grow and cost less. This trend will accelerate the communications and manufacturing trends described earlier. This trend could fundamentally change the nature of human values by eliminating manufacturing labor and making the content and delivery of education amazingly different. Computers will soon be able to recognize handwriting and speech, and translate into digital formats for either recording, transmitting or executing commands by machines. All of these data processing trends accelerate the demand for knowledge work at the expense of physical labor.

10. Financial integration of national economies will proceed as free trade integrates the global economy. Monetary sovereignty is the last power governments will part with (after all, what's a government worth that can't print money). Necessity will demand flexible exchange rate mechanisms. Jockeying for exchange rate advantages will result in evaluating national currencies in terms of a market basket of commodities. The recent spectacle of the European Community coming unglued over monetary policy and exchange rates prove these points. As the global economy evolves, and international financial and derivatives' markets expand, each nation will be at the mercy of the market in establishing the value of its currency. It will become more difficult for irresponsible governments to hide the fact they are using the printing press to confiscate wealth and dilute their money. Free trade exacerbates these trends.

11. The process of educating individuals will change radically. Education processes will be driven by the data processing and communications trends. The major obstacle to creating wealth in poor countries is lack of education. Despots fear the response of an educated citizenry. The use of interactive computers will improve the effectiveness and reduce the costs of education. A handful of compact discs will contain materials for a lifetime education. These trends will release the individuals involved in education to focus on the more complex and conceptual tasks that are difficult to automate. Education unions and "professional associations" that control the government sponsored education system will resist this trend ferociously. Economic benefits of these new services will overwhelm the parochial interests once the market discovers the technology. The "buggy whip" industry called public education will be replaced with new technology. Education will become efficient, effective and attractive to the student. This trend will make painfully visible the differences in cognitive ability among citizens and will require a fundamental re-examination of the concept of government-sponsored welfare.

12. Improvements in manufacturing technology and the trend to consume more goods as services will increase the importance of knowledge work. Japan is the first to recognize the inevitability of this trend, and is moving it's manufacturing operations off shore and preparing its youth for knowledge work. This trend cements the dependency between the manufacturing centers, typically poorer countries, and their knowledge based directors and owners. The consequence is the poorer countries in this partnership gradually grow richer, and become more knowledge based. The governments involved, on both sides of the partnership, can easily stifle this virtuous circle by blocking the market forces that drive the trend. Those Melds who advocate "deep ecology" are trying to destroy this trend in order to *reduce* the efficiency of manufacturing. They would use the force exclusivity of government to accomplish these ends. The majority of citizens would, if they new the dirty little secret, oppose the dilution of their wealth and happiness. The preachers of apocalypse have always had their following. The current generation of doomsayers is struggling to make their preaching a self-fulfilling prophecy by various acts of policy sabotage. America's "Environmental Protection Agency" is infiltrated with luddites. They are mandating and implementing measures that are causing more harm than good. The outlawing of chloroflourocarbons is a trillion dollar mistake. There was no substantial scientific data to support the predicted consequences of ozone depletion or the effects on the environment.

These trends and scenarios are well established. A government designer can rely on their continuation. There are other important trends that could turn one way or another depending on the course governments follow. The technology driven trends make the leverage government policies have much stronger. If we do not get it right this time, governments have the capacity for creating much greater mischief than at any time in the past. Saddam Hussein with a few nuclear weapons makes the point. The biological and physical sciences will make progress and the results will be disseminated. All civilized and responsible nations must be prepared to take action to neutralize the destructive forces of criminal governments. The trends described next all have the Damocles sword of rouge governments and ideological fanatics hanging over the outcome.

1. Disintegration of governments will become more frequent. Governments that were created by imperialistic traditions of force are particularly prone to come unglued as the forces that bound them are removed. The British and French empires disintegrated years ago. Ramifications are still felt. The Russian empire is the most recent one to go. The result has been an explosion of governments. The concept of empire is extinct. The world hopes that the Chinese maintain their traditional lack of enthusiasm for empire building. When the world is engaged in free trade, empires are not efficient unless their sole purpose is to extract tribute. This custom has gone into serious disfavor, due in no small part to the proliferation of modern armaments and communications. The likely trend is towards greater "value homogeneity" and smaller nations. Effective governments must accommodate fracturing nations. Governments cannot allow national disintegration to violate the welfare of their citizens. When the values in contention are religious or nationalistic dogma, the disintegration can become ugly and bloody. The future may contain more sovereign nations than now but they will not embrace empire building. They may proselytize their ideology. With open boarders, anyone could leave if they did not share those values. It is much easier to design a little government when all citizens share the same ideology and defensive weapons are affordable.

2. Governments can benefit their citizens by depending more on persuasion than force to build positive law. This is easier if: a) the governed nation is smaller and more value homogeneous and b) the government limits the number of functions it tries to perform. Insane and irrational ideologies can be tolerated in a small, homogeneous nation where most share the dementia. As this trend towards fracturing governments proceeds, it is essential that the rest of the world stop

those ideologies that engage in aggression and proselytizing. This may be accomplished by the United Nations or possibly by regional good Samaritans, after they consult with their neighbors. The empowerment of the UN with this task raises the specter of creating a bigger monster than was exorcised. The UN must never be given money to pay its own soldiers. As is now the custom, the UN can be armed with national forces, preferably all volunteer. Hand wringing over the conflicts in Eastern Europe's disintegration proves how difficult it is to come to grips with the monster of national disintegration. There is some small comfort in the fact that the artificial forces that glued these nations together in the first place created the mess. Sooner or later the lowest entropy state will return. There will be much bloodshed along the way if this is the solution the world selects. Rearranging people into value homogeneous nations is difficult. The use of ethnic cleansing to accomplish the goal is not an attractive approach. Everyone knows where he or she wants to go, but have no way of getting there.

3. Individual governments can become more centrist and Federalized, or can distribute their functions to lower levels of an organization. America has allocated more functions to the Federal government while diminishing the authority and resources of state and local governments. Governments can take on more or fewer functions. America's governments take on ever increasing functions. All of the experiments in government indicate that enormous inefficiency's are introduced when governments acquire more functions. European governments drove this road early on and are now scrambling to unload functions that have a huge cadre of dependents. There is little evidence to support the presumption that either central or local governments are more or less efficient. Both ends of the government organizational spectrum seem to foul up their functions with equal speed. An advantage lower levels of government have is they cannot print money. This advantage was challenged when California issued it's own money after they ran out of the real stuff.

4. Governments vary in their propensity to get involved in wars. If the trend in nations is more and smaller, and the trend in organization is toward central as opposed to dispersed, there will be more wars. This is not necessarily bad if the wars can be localized and limited to conventional weapons. War is an efficient means of settling conflict if the outcome is definitive and the conflict subsides with a consensus reached by the warring parties. The loss of human life is insignificant. The use of local wars to resolve ideological conflict is efficient and inexpensive compared to the alternatives. Intervention by larger nations to halt local conflicts has proven costly and ineffective. Intervention puts a cork in the bottle that later explodes when the underlying pressures build. If the smaller, value specialized nations incorporate religious or ideological elements in their charters, they are prone to war. Nuclear war, on a small scale, becomes probable as rocketry and missile guidance technology become available. A small amount of dedicated resources can put large population centers at risk. The only way to deal with such highly leveraged blackmail will be the resolute and swift application of massive force. Watching ones family and neighbors being slaughtered steels the most ardent pacifist for war. Within the next decade a major population center is likely to be destroyed or seriously damaged by a terrorist act utilizing a weapon of mass destruction. Every government should be making preparations and plans for this contingency, including the response to the perpetrator. If the New York Trade Center bomb had been Plutonium rather than airplanes, a more spectacular event would have commanded the public's attention. So far, Islamic terrorists have been reduced to "ankle nipping."

5. Civil disorder is created by a small fraction of the population. Governments can exacerbate this problem with policies. Strengthening private associations that instill values that preclude such behavior is a proven solution. It helps if the government sets a good example. Would the Oklahoma City federal building been bombed if the Waco massacre had not happened? Young males tend to be aggressive and violent. Psychiatrists and sociologists generate many theories to explain

why. In times of war, society uses these characteristics to the nations advantage. All societies have found the necessity to build into their customs and rules of behavior that control and channel these destructive impulses towards more constructive expression. Historical observations suggest that making entire sub-cultures dependent upon government wealth transfers destroys the mechanisms that keep destructive behavior in check. The creation of a zero-sum society rewards taking, not creating. Current government practices declared to help poorer segments of society have proven ineffective and destructive. The Roman circus proved better at solving this problem than does the modern welfare state. Expansive government laws that prohibit certain personal entertainments exacerbate the problem. Governments grab an ugly tiger by the tail when they choose to prohibit drugs, freedom of association or art forms. America's experience with prohibition of alcohol led to similar social disintegration, but has been forgotten. Drugs cause violence like wet sidewalks cause rain.

6. When governments take on functions that determine the quality or length of their citizen's lives, they take on the responsibility of placing quantitative value on life. Politicians that advocate government control of life saving functions deny this fact. They claim that the virtue of these actions is their egalitarianism. All will be treated "equally", but not necessarily "fairly." If a resource is scarce, there will be inequalities in its distribution. Heart transplants cannot be provided to everyone in need. Governments that have implemented nationalized health care have long waiting lists and some people are refused life saving procedures as a matter of policy. Government health care managers claim to impose "rational" planning. The implication is that scarce resources are allocated to maximize length and quality of life (whatever that means). "Rational" planning ignores the intrinsic inequity that results when the person who saved carefully so as to afford care in later life is denied while dedicating the resources to a 30 year old drug addict who drove his motorcycle into a tree. This is the tip of the iceberg. Glabs must place a quantitative value on human life by selecting which projects

they invest in or which positive law they enforce. Some functions of government demand that a quantitative comparison of the value of an individual's life be computed, either explicitly or implicitly. Many have the illusion that each human life is of infinite worth, and hence must be saved at any cost to the rest of society. This attitude flies in the face of economics and contradicts the reality of an often-brutal world. Social values have become completely wrapped around the axle because of the advocacy of special interests and egalitarian fools. When hundreds of thousands of dollars are spent saving a non-viable neonatal with a brain dead mother while healthy children go without inoculations, the resource miss-allocations must be considered criminal. Laws that allow enormous civil penalties when a physician fails in the attempt to save a life thwart human values. All of these examples place a defined and enforceable value on each life. Once the government assumes responsibility for allocating life saving resources, then government must determine who lives and who dies. The government implements these decisions, as they must, through the courts and the police. Authoritarianism is the only alternative to free markets. Some individuals consider the allocation created by market forces "unfair." Government sponsored alternatives are more distressing.

7. American governments have established a dogma that demands ideological adherence to the principle that genetics can have no role in decisions made by governments, individuals or courts. These ideological blinders are grotesque in their consequences. The perpetuation of this dogma causes despair and frustration. When a government bases decisions on the presumption that heritable traits cannot affect the outcome of an individual's fate, be it a prison term or grades in school, the foundation is laid for an incompetent and destructive result. This lie has been raised to a religious principle, and cannot be challenged; the emperor has no clothes. The Bell Curve enrages the politically correct. Discussing any relationship between intelligence and social performance is taboo. In America today, any suggestion that genes can have influence on individual performance is declared "Hitlerian." The con-

sequences of the rapidly increasing pool of knowledge about genetics must be taken into account. Negative and positive law must consider this knowledge. This places many difficult cecisions before government. The problems are made no simpler by denying the truth. Stalin's Soviet Union provides a historic lesson in the prominence and rise of T.D. Lyshenkov . Lyshenkov was a crackpot geneticist who stated that the genotype of a living plant or animal (including humans) could be changed by exposing the phenotype to appropriate environments. Stalin liked the consequences of such a science, and so he gave Lyschenkov complete freedom to liquidate all the established geneticists and replace them with his sycophants. One of many disastrous results was the destruction of Russian agricultural genetics. Consequences persist to this day. History will record as much damage to those societies that are now rejecting the truth of genetic sciences and statistics. Genetics will remain an emotion charged issue since each individual is so irreversibly affected. Government must not become the gatekeeper of this knowledge.

These seven trends will either continue or change depending on the kind of governments that are installed in the near future. Many of these trends pit the Melds against the Egons, and hence are difficult to resolve through consensus. Difficult is not impossible. The next chapter describes a Government that achieves consensus.

—the real bad guys

There are powerful forces at work that aim to annihilate modern technology, return the earth to primitive conditions and obliterate a large portion of the world's population. This nihilism is not what citizens want. Many follow the tune of these pied-pipers. Melds often, unwittingly, support this position by placing more power in the hands of those glabs dedicated to the cause. Equally destructive are those who advocate egalitarian outcomes of all social competitions. These Melds choose to eliminate the role of the market in allocating resources, replacing the market with a "fair" government bureaucracy. This group denies all knowledge and logic bestowed upon us by economics, history and genetic science. They pursue their agenda despite opposition by the great majority of citizens. These latter day pied pipers twist the time honored and workable principle of equality before the law to imply that there must be equality of results. These perverse ideologies must be heard in the marketplace of ideas. Some groups will embrace these concepts; they should be free to associate and advocate. When a small group of egalitarian, luddite fanatics attempt to seize power from an inattentive Republic by perverting law and government associations to their ends, it must stop.

The Government architecture described in the last chapter provides ample opportunity for all groups to advocate and practice their ideologies and values, but constrains their effect to the group that sympathizes. The philosophies of Meld and Egon are in conflict. The goal of government should be allow individuals to achieve their values, not to select winners and losers.

CHAPTER 8

▼

RISK MANAGEMENT

And almost every one when age,
Disease, or sorrows strike him,
Inclines to think there is a God,
Or something very like Him.

—Arthur Hugh Clough

As recently as 100 years ago, there were no interventions that could significantly prolong human life. Crude but effective tools for terminating life were widely used. A visit to the physician offered only palliatives, not a significant probability of life extension.

Modern technology has provided tools to overcome the life shortening effects of disease and wounds. Some of these interventions are costly. Most citizens will reach a time in their life that medical intervention could prolong their life for years, months or days. With the encouragement of demagogic politicians, citizens have become convinced that they are *entitled* to these life-extending interventions, regardless of cost. This state of affairs presents an enormous dilemma for a government of consensus. This dilemma is part of a larger issue of allocating and reducing *risks,* whether created by government actions or natural events.

Risks abound. When we drive our automobile, travel on an airplane, or go the beach, there are many harmful events that could occur *because* we engaged in these acts. Some risks are subtle and are generally ignored by most citizens. A terrorist could deliver a weapon of mass destruction to your city. This possibility has progressed from the remote to the probable. An undetected asteroid could impact the earth and cause monumental damage, possibly reducing the number of humans to a fraction of the current population. Some citizens are equally worried about the risk to other animal life forms.

Determining the *best* trade among risks is a personal value. The issue of abortion is extraordinarily contentious, but this issue also is a risk related decision. Whether a woman's body is the property of the state or her own, the decision to abort a fetus is a trade-off among risks. These risks will play out, regardless of any intervention by the state. If the mother-to-be is sufficiently poor, the fate of her offspring could be horrible. If she lives in a third world country that starves a large part of its citizens each year, the offspring could suffer a fate worse than not being born. But the essential issue is who makes the risk related decisions; the mother, the government, the church? And does the association that influences the risk decision also take responsibility for the outcome; i.e. caring for the unwanted and unsupported child. It is evident from all we see around us that individual lives are *not* of infinite worth, to be preserved at any cost to society. This notion, leading to the above-described conundrums, is a viscous falsehood perpetrated by religious fanatics whose only goal can be to terminate civilization, as we know it. The greens who want to preserve any piece of "nature" at "any cost" is akin to the right-to-life luddites who contend that society must intervene to save any potential for human life. The absurdity of both positions is unbounded, and most citizens, if presented the facts, would agree.

Before effective medical intervention was available, life and death amounted to a roll of the dice. The prudent could avoid unnecessary dangers, but once the death card was dealt, there was little hope of a re-deal. This state of affairs led to a fatalistic attitude and encouraged mysticism and religion as tools to help avert catastrophe. Regardless of the value one placed on a human or animal life, there was little to be accomplished, even with massive resources, to cheat fate once a disease or wound was inflicted. In the case of disease, there was little knowledge to help one avoid contracting the ailment; it appeared to be a random phenomena.

In the last 50 years the potential for risk management and abatement has changed profoundly. This change has led to a major readjustment of human values and the role individuals expect the government to play in controlling risk. In many cases, the government has become the ultimate arbiter of how risk is allocated among the citizens—literally the government controls who lives or dies. The technology that makes this possible has provided enormous benefits by increasing the length and quality of human lives. This medical technology, coupled with improved agricultural technology has allowed an enormous growth in population.

Before effective intervention existed, it was easy, if not irresistible, for religious and political leaders to tell their subjects that they had infinite respect for their lives and would go to any length to save them. Knowing full well that nothing could be done to extend a single life, the leaders were never called to task. New technology has changed all of that; leaders are now expected to put your money where their mouth is. The availability of risk reduction techniques is widely recognized by the citizens. They expect the government to provide risk reduction services. Of course, a willing bureaucracy has bellied up to the bar for this challenge: the Environmental Protection Agency, the public health sycophants, emergency relief organizations, the Superfund and on and on. Unfortunately, most of these government programs are based on pseudo-science and faulty rationale. The efforts sponsored by governments have led to massively inefficient allocation of resources devoted to risk reduction. Since citizen's hopes have been elevated beyond reason, a major challenge for a consensus government is to back away from many risk allocation roles. Those risk reduction activities that can be rationalized for government intervention must be based on solid cost-benefit analyses and not pseudo-science. This effort will require no less than a calculus of the value of life that a substantial majority of citizens can accept as valid and representing their values. Achieving this goal will require careful thought and broad debate.

Governments intervene to achieve the "proper" allocation of risks in a variety of ways. The law can be used to create regulations that prevent individuals or enterprises from certain activities that might create risks. Product design laws are similar. The government can sell insurance at below market rates to alleviate risks. Bureaucracies can be established to oversee industries or activities. All of these techniques are widely used by governments at all levels to achieve risk abatement or re-allocation. Some may be sensibly performed by governments, most are not.

Events that cause human suffering are many and varied. There are government programs to avoid or re-distribute the cost of such events. Partial lists of events governments intervene to ameliorate are:

- Spread of contagious disease

- Food poisoning/toxicity

- Aircraft and flight safety

- Automobile accidents and injuries

- Weather caused damage

- Earthquake caused damage

- Unemployment

- Inherited or birth defects

- Chemical and radioactive toxicity

- Childhood injuries

- Adverse effects of therapeutic and recreational drugs

- Medical care

- Ascetic damage to environments

- Fire damage.

In most cases private insurers and tort laws can adequately deal with these risks. Many of the government interventions distort markets by subsidizing risky behavior, such as building houses in earthquake or hurricane prone areas.

Science can predict the cause and incidence of many calamitous events. While technology has certainly added to the list of modern risks (airplane crashes, nuclear war, adverse drug reactions, etc.) the vast majority of citizens believe the benefits outweigh the risks. In most cases, the individual is free to avoid the risk if they don't accept the trade-off. Many of the events that was once considered random and unexplainable are now either preventable or can be statistically forecast with precision. The scientific method of determining cause and effect relationships is a powerful tool in risk abatement. It is also a tool that many academic and bureaucratic organizations and individuals have perverted to their personal gain. The excellent little book by Steven Milloy explains how the pseudo-science of associating an environmental event with a particular risk is perverted to assure continued funding of useless studies and abatement programs. The total lack of evidence to establish real cause and effect of the harm of Alar, dioxin, electromagnetic radiation, perfume, second hand smoke, etc. has not impeded the environmental Nazis. The government is helpless to defend against such non-scientific nonsense since rationality is not an accepted tool of politics. The public health bureaucracy previously devoted to fighting diseases such as tuberculosis and cholera compounds the problem. Now that their original mission has essentially disappeared, they seek new employment opportunities by searching for remote health correlations such as second hand tobacco smoke and gun ownership. The new threat of bio-terrorism may rejuvenate their original mission.

Governments enter the risk management business by two methods; direct actions to reduce risk and financial compensation to those who have had, or are likely to have, misfortune. Hundreds of examples can be provided for each technique. Direct actions include regulations to improve the safety of everything from automobiles to toys. The national weather service, the department of agriculture meat inspection and the center for disease control, to name a few, provide direct services. These services are performed by glabs and aim to reduce the probability of injury, sickness or death. Direct financial compensation can be paid in the form of emergency loans, direct payments to disabled individuals, subsidizing or underwriting insurance at a loss, and on and on. Of course, there are many private charities that compete with the government for victims. Massive amounts of money are donated to these groups every year, with most of the proceeds going to the fund raising professionals. At least the government does not suffer this overhead expense; they simply seize the assets required to fund their risk abatement programs.

What does risk management have to do with designing the Government? The government, by its nature, cannot perform risk abatement efficiently. Worse yet, by attempting to provide such services they destroy consensus and pit one group of citizens against another. In those cases where individuals have suffered losses, there is likely a consensus to provide emergency relief or long term welfare benefits where appropriate. This kind of abatement transfers wealth from the more fortunate to the unlucky, and is best performed at the lower levels of government organization. All other attempts to reduce risk by government are totally misguided and are much better resolved by tort law and private insurers. A few examples will explain why.

Subsidizing or underwriting insurance that is not profitable for private concerns (earthquake, hurricane, flood insurance) simply distorts markets for the real estate involved and encourages individuals to take risks that they otherwise would not take. If someone wants to build their house on an earthquake fault, why should more prudent taxpayers subsidize this foolishness? Why should the government mandate safety standards for every conceivable product when the manufacturers are exposed to legal actions if their products are harmful? Federal mandates often provide a layer of immunity to the industry since the government has effectively indemnified them by dictating design. Often the government mandated measures are not cost-effective, and result in enormous indirect costs to the consumer. In those cases where services are performed, the marketplace can provide them more cost-effectively if there is a demand for them. Except for providing appropriate cash payments to the unfortunate, there is no risk abatement activity that the government need perform. The result of government meddling in risk abatement usually results in economic loss.

▼

CHAPTER 9

THE SOLUTION

"unhappily a written form of government is not a Gibraltar that can resist the waves, but a sandy beach, which, while it seems to beat back the devouring waters, is always losing in the struggle. Each decade sees some principle of the Constitution either weakened or nullified, and the difficulty is that the people are only sensible of their peril after the principle is destroyed, and when it is too late to restore it"

—James M. Beck

—*something old, something new*

Governments have degraded and robbed their citizens for centuries. Even those governments that started out with the right principles evolve into autocratic, imperious monsters. The great American Republic was the least offensive government in the world. Many observers noted the fragility of this arrangement and warned Americans to stay on their guard against those events that have now occurred. It is not enough to know what went wrong. We must fix the problem. Unfortunately, we cannot stop and start over. The special interests that live off the government's redistributed wealth have grown into a powerful coalition of forces. The Soviet Union is to be admired for their heroic attempt to rid themselves of an oppressive government. Can America exhibit the same heroism?

This chapter describes a Government that will work. The architecture is simple. Making the transition to the Government will not be. The longer the political rot persists, the harder it will be to exorcise.

The Government is as close to the American government as possible. There are two reasons for clinging to the American model. First, it worked well in its purer historic form and has a good track record. Second, the transition to a new government will be easier if changes are minimal. The changes could be achieved with a few constitutional amendments and the election of a president and congress that would implement the Government. These changes would not violate the intent of the founders, but would bring the original American concept in line with modern technology, world affairs and demographics. It is no surprise that the enormously successful American experiment in government should require some fine-tuning after 200 years of service

The aging of America's republican political system has been graceful. The last 200 years have evolved a severe imbalance in political power. Vested interests and panoply of corruption mechanisms extract a heavy and unaffordable toll on the citizens. Parallels to the Soviet experience are alarming. As the human body is unable to accurately reproduce its cells as they age, American governments have lost their ability to regenerate the fundamental safeguards essential to the founder's vision. It is time to correct these problems.

The foundation of Government is the constitution. In the original American constitution, the negative law is expressed in the first ten amendments; tacked on at the end almost as an afterthought. The body of the constitution is devoted primarily to describing the organization and rules of succession of the government; this structure is sound and well tested. There are minor defects in the existing constitution. Negative law should be the centerpiece of the constitution, not addenda. The clear and concise principles stated in America's constitution have been eroded and circumvented by imperious judges and legislators. These glabs value an ideology or project more than the law. The Government prevents such heresy by requiring the high court to administer only the negative law. A network of judicial and police structures enforce the negative law by preventing other units of government from violating negative law or implementing positive law that contradicts the negative law. The major change in the charter of the high court is that they only decide whether a legislative act violates negative law. They are not empowered to create positive law by judicial decree. This leads to the third and final axiom upon which the Government is based:

Axiom 3—Negative law always takes precedence over positive law.

Three axioms provide the foundation for a workable government:

AXIOM 1—Government will take no actions that interfere with individual efforts that do not cause physical or economic harm to others unless such efforts were a result of prior agreement between the parties involved.

AXIOM 2—Governments will take the actions necessary to prevent individuals from using force, or the credible threat of force, to harm or achieve efforts not intended or desired by a citizen. The exception to this axiom is the police force established by the government. The police may use force or intimidation to achieve behavior compliance.

AXIOM 3—Negative law always takes precedence over positive law.

These three axioms can provide the foundation for a government of consensus. If an individual insists that a dogma or personal interests take precedence over these principles, then it is unlikely that individual could accept consensus government. Such individuals accept continued conflict for principle or greed. The overwhelming majority of citizens want a consensus building and creating government, not a zero-sum anarchy of taking.

These axioms of Government implicitly distinguish positive and negative law. The negative law rests in the constitution and is stated in a few paragraphs. Government assures citizens they are free to move about the country as they choose, to write and publish what they want and to own wealth. Citizens are assured consistent treatment by the law enforcement function and they can vote. If the interpretation of a proposed law requires a positive law be enforced to achieve conformance with the proposed law, then the proposed law must be interpreted as positive. If Government tries to create a right that requires seizure of property, this right must be interpreted as positive law and therefore enacted under the constraints for creating positive law.

A Government structure is now defined that is consistent with these axioms. The implementation of this Government will provide satisfaction of most citizen's values. There is no claim for uniqueness; there may be alternative or better Government designs that will be discovered in the future. The Government design will work, and is a vast improvement over the current situation. The effort required to achieve this change is enormous; perhaps impossible.

—the Government

Once the Government is established, it is imperative that it not again evolves into a quagmire of vested interests. To prevent this, the highest judicial authority is structured and empowered to assure that negative law remains intact and enforced. This high court is expressly forbidden by the constitution from implementing, either directly or by interpretation, any positive law. The high court cannot render a decision that requires the allocation or reallocation of government or private resources. The higher judicial system has no function other than to assure that the negative law is respected and obeyed. All positive law will be created at the lowest levels of government organization, and cannot become a subject of higher levels of government until a majority of subsidiary units have adopted such positive law. The Pandora's box that was opened when the Supreme Court decided that the "commerce clause" of the U.S. constitution provided justification for federal involvement in nearly any citizen's affairs must be closed.

The creation of positive law is severely constrained. Elected leaders cannot expand it in response to a vested interest or the promise of personal gain. Positive law imposes constraints on Type 1 behavior and redistributes confiscated wealth. All positive law will be created democratically by the use of modern communications and data processing technology. Citizens will vote directly on each positive law. The same process selects leaders. Each citizen qualified to vote will have a unique identification number, like a credit card, that is encoded for error correction and security requirements. The citizens can vote by telephone, mail or with a computer terminal. The telephone system would be automated. The voice response system will repeat the vote to verify that no entry errors were made. Privacy issues must be dealt with in order to assure that the identification system cannot be accessed by any other government function and thereby correlated to other government records. An elite corps of glabs would be recruited and trained, like the cadres of military personnel who man strategic weapon launch centers, to maintain the integrity and security of the voting system. This function of Government is the most critical and important of all. Those responsible for maintaining the voting system have placed in their hands the highest public trust; violation of this trust must be treated as treason and punished accordingly. Any attempt to defraud or interfere with the voting system would be punishable by death.

The elected leaders will have a more modest task. They may introduce positive law for vote by the effected set of citizens, and they may decide on the magnitude of the majority vote required for passage. The range of majorities the legislature can approve will be constrained by the constitution. All positive law would require at least a 50% majority for passage. Statistical methods could be used for selecting a magnitude of the plurality required by defining a "three sigma" level of assuring the voters desires are achieved. Positive law is always introduced at the lowest level of government that it effects. When a majority of lower level government units have approved the law, it can be introduced for approval at the next higher unit. A county or city would be the first unit to approve a new positive law. When a majority of citizens in a majority of cities and counties within a state had approved that law, it could be introduced for the states citizens to approve. Since the legislators will have reduced responsibilities, their salaries are reduced to reflect these responsibilities.

All citizens can vote via telephone or computer. Each month the text of all positive laws that were approved for vote will be published. The laws proposed are made available through electronic and printed media. A period of several months would be allowed for the vote unless the issue was time critical (e.g. flood relief, defensive actions from a foreign invasion). Anyone can change his or her vote up to the deadline. This method of creating positive law will place a premium on keeping the text of the law simple and concise. In those states that allow referendums to create law, the laws proposed are usually expressed in a paragraph, or at most a page of text. The Government would never approve hundreds of pages of legalese.

The national government maintains the data processing and communication system to support the voting process. Building and maintaining the voting system is the primary responsibility of the federal government. All levels of government use the service. Issues are put on the ballot by any political jurisdiction, from a small town to the federal government. Each citizen can vote on any issue within his jurisdiction, with those votes cast through the central voting machine. Rigorous statistical sampling of voters would verify the integrity of the system. The data processing systems are redundant and highly protected. All data transfer functions are protected by error correction and security maintenance techniques. The flawless performance of airline reservation and financial systems proves the technical feasibility of this technology. The system would be freer of error than existing manual systems run by incompetent and often corrupt local glabs. The cost savings would be substantial. No time would be lost going to voting places and government employment could be reduced.

Any individual is free to introduce a positive law for vote by the citizens. They can use any media to advocate the issue. The advocate would have to obtain a minimum level of voter approval before going to the ballot. Statistical sampling methods could be economically implemented to verify that proposed legislation was of sufficient interest to warrant the expense of placing the legislation in the voting queue. The advocate must pay for the costs of introducing the proposition into the central distribution and voting system. No positive law can violate or interfere with negative law. If a law is so challenged, the courts would decide.

This system allows each citizen to participate in creating positive law. This process creates a burden that many citizens would not want to suffer. If citizens had to study and vote on each issue, they might choose to not bother. This leaves the decisions to those few who had an overriding interest. This is not desirable since vested interests could exert extraordinary influence; although not as much as the current system.

There is a solution to this problem. The solution is similar to the creation of political parties, but keeps control in the hands of the citizens rather than party leaders. The constitution provides for the creation of associations that can vote for citizens on all or a particular range of issues. Each citizen could join, or give his power of attorney to associations that represent values consistent with his own. The citizen could join an association empowered to cast all of his votes, or he could join several specialized associations empowered to cast his vote on one category of issue. All positive laws would be categorized so ambiguity could not arise in assigning issues to associations. These associations are free to solicit voter's participation as political parties do today. Citizens could withdraw or change their voting associations at any time. Severe penalties would be due anyone tampering with or failing to disclose voting records of the association. The voting associations could represent broad philosophical positions or dedicate themselves to a narrow range of issues, such as trade law or environmental law. A citizen could join multiple associations, but when doing so would have to declare their priority in the event two different associations were voting on the same issue. This complexity would be impossible for a manual system but is easily accomplished by available data processors. The associations could be financed by for profit groups, by a few large contributors, or by not-for profit associations. Since the associations voting record is always visible to the members, and the member can withdraw at any time, the tyranny of the two party system is gone. The Democratic and Republican parties would be free to continue their existence under these new rules. They would probably have to become more explicit on the issues and vote more consistently in representing these positions if they are to survive. This method of creating political associations would assure that each citizen could implement his basic values effectively without spending inordinate amounts of time studying the issues and candidates presented. This process would force the system to focus on principles rather than issues. The system achieves all the advantages of a multi-party advocacy without opening the door for vested interests to plunder the public purse.

Positive law is introduced and enacted at the lowest level of government organization that has not enacted that law previously. *This princi-*

ple is critical to the success of Government. The federal government could not introduce any positive law until a majority of states had approved. A state could not introduce a positive law until all counties had approved. This system of "subsidiary" would result in simpler laws since differences in wording or nuance could force a restart at the lower level of government. Creating positive law that benefits few at the expense of everyone is the major occupation of congress. Instead of letting the largest unit of government dictate wealth redistribution, this task will be the responsibility of the smaller units of government; the town, the city, the county. A town in Maine is unlikely to vote a subsidy for millionaire sugar farmers in Louisiana. Most jurisdictions will not abandon charity. Concern for the "poor" is likely to be the first cry of opposition. Everyone is free to move to a different jurisdiction if the legal environment is not satisfying.

The principle of relegating the creation of positive law to the lowest levels of government organization is essential to achieving a consensus between Meld and Egon. A small unit of government may become egalitarian, like the Mennonite and Amish enclaves that exist within other units of local governments. As long as these units are not violent proselytizers, they can comfortably co-exist with the larger civil society. The constitutional amendment required to strengthen this principle is a derivative of the current constitution which delegates to the states those powers not explicitly delegated to the federal government. The European Community introduced this principle of "subsidiarity" into their constitution. The central government does not undertake any function that can be accomplished by a member country (even if the member country should choose not to undertake that function). Unfortunately, Europe has honored this concept more in the breach. In so doing, the European Union has doomed itself to a government of *taking* and conflict forever. The EU has become little more than a boil on the ass of European democracy.

The important elements of the Government have now been described. Most readers have formed an opinion on the viability and desirability of the Government. The Meld reader might react negatively to the thought of establishing his dogma from the "ground up." This seems a small price too pay for the freedom to practice a favorite dogma. Except in America, the Melds haven't been winning many battles lately. It is unlikely the Egon will feel overly threatened by Meld dogma if it is limited in scope and requires direct approval by fellow citizens. The marketplace of ideas will reign supreme.

Describing the opposition best reveals the consequences of the Government. The most vigorous opposition is expected from the vested interests that profit from the current system of pork barrel politics. Even these participants can conceive of a positive benefit from abandoning their place at the public trough; namely self-respect. Both Melds and Egons should be able to appreciate the elimination of the influence of vested interests that plunder the public purse without regard to ideology.

Most positive law is likely to be repealed. Laws that favor or protect a small group of vested interests will be discarded. Citizens will have the opportunity to redistribute their wealth, but first on a local level. Fast legislative response to disasters or special needs can be provided by this system. Private associations such as churches or charities are free to use the wealth released to do good works as they see fit. Americans have never been niggardly.

Positive laws that deal with complex subjects have uncertain outcomes. The government allows all citizens to vote on positive law that is international in character. Tariffs, international navigation rights and entering war are legitimate subjects for vote at the national level. It is possible that citizens would approve of specific welfare measures to alleviate the unemployment caused by lower tariff barriers in order to gain the benefits of lower cost imported goods. Once the economic facts of the matter are exposed, rational outcomes will prevail. Citizens can make mistakes just as do government leaders. The major difference is that mistakes can be quickly corrected.

—what next?

Transition to the Government does not require fundamental changes in the structure of the American government. The Government would reduce government's functions and size. The established political parties will be bitterly opposed to these changes. Implementation of the Government will require a new political association. A majority of the new association members must be elected to both houses of congress. This will not be easy. The Democratic and Republican parties would bring enormous resources to bear against the Government. Their strangle hold on campaign contributions, salaries and perks would be in jeopardy. The movement that Ross Perot created proved the willingness of the electorate to break away from established parties and attach their loyalties to a new grass roots movement. The cost of mounting Perot's modest campaign was enormous.

The first step must be to get the attention of the voters and structure a clear path they can follow to the creation of Government. This path could begin by assembling a constitutional convention of like-minded individuals under a leader who can organize, coordinate and motivate the group to generate a draft of amendments to the constitution. The new constitution can be debated and used as a beacon for the new party's campaign.

The supreme court might present an obstacle, but not an insurmountable one. Their role in Government would be precisely what the founders had in mind. The high court has strayed far from their original charter, becoming social activists and allowing glabs to bend the meaning of the constitution to suite their collectivist needs. Perhaps a wide consensus of citizens would cause the sages to reconsider their positions and abandon social activism for simply enforcing negative law. The route of impeachment of justices is always available, but hopefully unnecessary. All members of the Supreme Court need do is act like lawyers instead of politicians or ideologues. Anyone seeking this exalted position would have to read and memorize the new constitution; legal training is not a prerequisite.

The implementation of foreign policy would be much as it is now. The executive would take initiatives. The executive would staff the bureaucracy and maintain communications with other countries' governments. The method of establishing policy must be changed. Instead of secret agendas generated in the back rooms of the State Department, the decisions and their rationale would be disclosed to the citizens. These changes would be consistent with the constitution of the founders. If the executive, as commander in chief, chose to deploy troops outside national boundaries to engaging in combat, he would have to seek approval of the voters. If a surprise attack a la W.W.II occurred, the president as commander in chief could engage in defensive actions immediately. The commander in chief could proceed for 90 days as he saw fit until a plebiscite gave him approval for expanding hostilities as required defeating the invader.

Assuring the integrity of negative law and defending the country are handled in extraordinary ways. The success of these two functions is imperative to the survival of Government. All other issues are of less import, and can be dealt with by a process described next.

Achieving transition to the Government without causing severe disruption or exposing the country to dangers is the major challenge. Witnessing the attempts of the communist countries converting to liberal governments proves the dangers and pitfalls that a transition can impose. Fortunately America has a structure of liberal government in place, and still has a reasonably free market for ideas. If we can't do it, no one can. The great leap of faith is that the citizens can collectively decide what is best for their own welfare. These citizens must support a system of negative law that protects basic rights of their fellow citizens; even when such protection causes some individual's loss or obstacles to gain. The biggest losers will be lawyers and politicians; a loss the citizens can probably tolerate. The greatest challenge is to re-awaken the ability of the citizen to reason and apply this to achieve an understanding of the *real* consequences of alternatives presented for vote.

—*probable outcomes*

The Government places significant power in the hands of citizens. Predicting the precise outcome is difficult, but a significant reduction in positive law is certain. Some likely outcomes are predicted below. There is no mechanism for any group of citizens to do great mischief. If a bad positive law is passed, it is easy for the citizens to correct once the consequences are evident. America is now burdened with massive amounts of legislation that had either perverse effects or did not achieve the intended purpose. Yet legislators never repeal any legislation; it seems as if their collective pride of authorship can't allow the rejection of old laws. This legislative cancer will not effect the Government.

Initiating warfare for purposes other than direct defense of the nation is a decision that profoundly affects all citizens. A direct attack on the nation is a fundamentally different issue, and the executive can and should have the freedom of action to respond immediately. The chief executive's ability to lead effectively in these circumstances would hopefully be a major consideration in his election. Surprise attack is not the circumstance in which most warfare has been initiated in America's history. The Government is structured to make extra territorial application of force a decision by referendum and approved by 2/3 of the voters. The purposes of the proposed deployment can be humanitarian aid, meeting treaty obligations, or protecting some mystical "national interest'; it does not matter. Negative law would prohibit the drafting of troops by the national militia. The nation must get soldiers by enthusiasm for the cause or raising the wages. This may give rouge governments a telegraphic warning of national intent. A vote of 2/3ds of the citizens to support a war against, say North Korea, sends a powerful message of deterrence. Would Saddam Hussein have invaded Kuwait if the American citizens had voted to intervene? He would certainly have done so if the vote were negative. The result would have been the end of one despotic government and its replacement by another. If the vote for going to war with Saddam were positive, the arguments would have to be made on the basis of national interests, not the demonizing of a petty dictator.

International trade has a major impact on American citizens. Trade issues affect economic well being. If we allow the lesser-developed countries to sell us their goods, they become wealthier. Rich countries can achieve greater security by increasing the wealth of the impoverished. Increased wealth makes citizens of poor countries less likely to immigrate and less likely to be duped into war by their leaders. The executive branch of Government would negotiate trade agreements and submit them for approval by the citizens. A majority must approve the negotiated agreement. A law could expand negotiated agreements unilaterally if it did not violate the approved agreements. The high court would decide issues of conflict in negotiated treaties. A complex example is the case of the U.S. prohibiting importation of tuna that was caught in nets that killed dolphin. A group of environmental activists, soon joined by US tuna fisherman, proposed this legislation. Was this an artificial trade barrier against imported tuna, or was it an issue of national environmental sovereignty? This decision is appropriate for the high court since it involves international treaty interpretation.

The outcome of specific votes on trade agreements and minimum wage laws is hard to predict. Citizens are torn between the evils of job losses and the good of reduced consumer prices and/or higher wages. Most realize that trade makes poor countries richer so they can buy our goods. This problem is not simple, nor should it be treated so. Economists, lawyers and politicians debate these issues endlessly with no consensus. Vested interests will work vigorously to sway citizens' votes on these matters. Wise decisions are more likely to come from citizens than from congress. As manufacturing processes become more automated and flexible and wages come more to equilibrium throughout the world, the movement of manufactured goods between countries will become less advantageous. New trade issues will revolve around knowledge and information. Protection of intellectual property will become more important than trade barriers. Trade issues as we know them today are likely to fade into the background as country's gear for competition in the knowledge and services sectors. What does McDonalds really bring to Moscow except knowledge about how to make French fries, grow beef, formulate catsup and train staff?

There is variability in local laws that prohibit "first person" or victimless crimes. Prohibitions against drug use, prostitution, pornography etc. have been mandated from both the top down and the bottom up. The federal government prohibits some drug use and controls and discourages other drugs such as alcohol. Local communities sort out their tolerance for prostitution and pornography. The bottoms up approach has proven to work infinitely better, and hence the federal laws relating to drug prohibition would become null and void until all lower jurisdictions voted for them. To be sure, modern telecommunications and transportation systems make a "bottoms up" approach to some ideological prohibitions difficult. Some argue that such laws are necessary because citizens who consume drugs create antisocial and criminal acts. This argument is specious. There are many laws to prosecute those antisocial acts. Evidence indicates it is prohibition that creates the violence. If there were an open market for the drugs, with the government taxing them and requiring accurate labeling, there would be little violence caused by drugs. Drug related violence is insignificant compared to alcohol related traffic deaths and injuries. Small, tight knit and value homogeneous communities could propose laws against first person crimes. They might be passed by a majority of voters. A small, vocal group of megalomaniac moralists would not be able to move congress to pass such laws that effect everyone in the nation. However many communities passed such laws, the federal government would be kept out of the business. This would release a massive amount of resources now engaged in the spurious "war on drugs." Individuals would be free to move, or at least vacation to places which did not outlaw their favorite pastime. A desire to gamble leads citizens to travel to Nevada or Atlantic City. An example of the hypocrisy of governments is state legislatures who once saw gambling as an immoral and sinful pastime but now sees government sponsored gambling as honorable and taxable. In order to assure that their citizens are less corrupted by state sponsored gambling, the lotteries offer lower odds to pay off than do competitive private casinos.

The environment is an appropriate subject for government involvement. Potential benefits to society can include reduced health maintenance costs and esthetics. There are many opportunities to improve our environment, government must set priorities and decide which projects will be funded with the resources made available by the citizens. This process is best approached rationally. Glabs can analyze the relative benefits and costs of alternatives. The environmental "movement" has unfortunately become the hiding place for collectivists who could not achieve the welfare state or the nationalization of enterprises by their political persuasion. These political watermelons (green on the outside and pink on the inside) hope to achieve their goals by pleading the necessity of environmental salvation. This dangerous subterfuge must be stopped. Environmental measures should be approved by a simple majority of those citizens directly affected by the measure. Any individual, or the legislature, proposing environmental legislation, must also propose an affected jurisdiction. Any contest of this jurisdiction would be decided in the courts before the vote took place. A single vote would approve or disapprove all elements of existing federal legislation. Authorized voters are those directly affected. Establishing jurisdictions would be cumbersome; but no more so than the legal morass created by environmental impact statements, endangered species acts, wet lands acts, etc. If a measure effected the wet-lands in North Carolina, it would be voted on only by the citizens of North Carolina. Air pollution measures in Los Angeles would be decided by those effected, not by the EPA and congress. Government taking of private property to satisfy environmental goals must be fully compensated. Costs are disclosed through the budgetary process. There would be no free ride for environmental enthusiasts who want the world as their park.

Mandates by the government are positive law. Mandates force the allocation of resources by those not participating in the alleged benefits. As the federal government has found themselves short of resources, they resort to mandates that require other jurisdictions to do their bidding. No funding is provided to carry out the mandate. The federal government's requirements for states to inspect automobiles for emissions in a particular manner, or to force limited commuting hours, or to educate and provide health care for illegal immigrants are all examples of legislative arrogance and irresponsibility.

Redistribution of wealth is positive law. Redistribution includes cash benefits, guarantees of loans, selective tax exclusion and subsidized or forced insurance underwriting. If 50 % of the population perceives they will benefit from redistribution, that 50% might exercise a tyranny of the majority. To prevent this tyranny a substantial majority must approve all wealth transfer or redistribution laws. The positive laws are introduced at the lowest level of government organization and approved by a majority of subordinate jurisdictions. Before a positive law can be introduced to a higher jurisdiction, it must have been approved by a majority of lower ones.

Negative law protects property. If a democracy degenerates to voting for the redistribution of the wealthy's assets to the 51% majority, anarchy is near. This is the intellectual equivalent of justifying mobs looting stores because they did not have sufficient funds to buy the products therein. This position has been publicly defended by many Melds.

The smaller unit of government would approve welfare legislation more readily than the larger. Charity begins at home. A poor community may provide less generous benefits, but benefits in keeping with their standard of living. It is unlikely that any community would want their welfare benefits to encourage and subsidize drug addiction and teen age pregnancy. Foreign welfare would be treated in the same manner, except that the entire national population would vote foreign aid after introduction by the federal legislature. Private charity is always available if a minority feels strongly about helping starving Africans or defenseless Israeli's.

Nations that adopt the Government are likely to become smaller, not larger. The Government must provide a workable and non-violent mechanism to allow nations to fracture. If part of the nation decides it is better off succeeding from the larger government, they must be given that opportunity. This idea goes against federalism. The ballot better resolves a reasonable escape valve for intransigent groups than warfare or oppression. Squaring accounts with infrastructure investments and defense considerations is a problem. The seceding unit must not get a "free ride" on defense or infrastructure at the expense of the original government. This issue is complex. The USSR's break up demonstrates how serious these problems are and how they can be resolved. The freedom to fracture national governments would be extended to allowing the elimination of layers of government. Such actions will meet with equally fierce resistance by the employees whose jobs are jeopardized. If the Government is implemented in America, the 21st century could see a North American continent populated by a dozen or more nations. Quebec may lead this trend.

Governments have always been attracted to enterprise. As a moth drawn to a flame, governments believe that they can solve short-term problems of unemployment, labor strife, and unequal distribution of wealth with government run enterprise. The motives for government control of enterprise are usually vile, not noble. The results of government run enterprise have been uniformly tragic for the citizens. Based on these lessons, any unit of government that proposes to engage in enterprise must gain 2/3 of the effected citizens' votes. Enterprise includes any activity in which the government will invest, manage, create profit or loss, or produce goods or services. It is difficult to predict the citizens' decisions in activities such as the post office and mortgage insurance. If the costs and benefits are exposed it is likely that they will turn to the private sector. The government's role in regulating enterprise is different from engaging in enterprise. Regulatory laws are treated as redistribution issues. Regulation attempts to force internalization of social costs that are avoided by the industry in question.

The type and degree of punishment for crime varies widely among cultures. An important value of society is their discomfort with antisocial behavior. Killing a fellow citizen is frowned on. The circumstances may dictate the punishment. A person who has a stroke while driving and kills five kindergarten students is viewed differently than the recidivist rapist who kidnaps, rapes and strangles a teen-age girl. Punishments meted out for particular crimes are best left to citizens. The political process turns into a punishment frenzy when a crime provides opportunities for politicians to meet the press. While citizens may make some temporary errors in defining punishments, they can be quickly corrected. Everyone soon discovers that $1 parking tickets result in massive traffic congestion. The imagination of the citizenry will find appropriate punishment for villains who rape and strangle little girls.

The issue of government budgets is complex. Politicians have tried to obscure budget issues so they could hide pet projects. They know citizens will not approve such projects, so they hide them in protected pockets of budget that are popular. Citizens cannot do a worse job of budget making than the current government.

Budgets are created in two categories. First, each piece of positive law would have an associated price tag. The sponsor would propose a budget for the activity. If the law was approved, the budget could not be exceeded without another vote. Second, the administrative cost of running the various layers of government must be paid. This category of budget pays for enforcing the law. The elected politicians then in power define these costs. Any challengers could propose changes to this budget. If the challenger won he could not exceed that budget. When voting for a leader, you vote for his administrative budget. If he exceeds that budget, he is immediately dismissed without further pay and another election is held for the remainder of his term. Small variances would be allowed for unexpected emergencies. The budget could be amended by a vote if unusual circumstances arise. This constraint placed on elected leaders is no more demanding than that placed on any private sector manager or household.

Major categories of budget would be voted on directly by the citizens. Defense, welfare, foreign aid and other major functions would be proposed by the units of government and approved or discarded. If not approved, the budget could be reduced and re submitted for a vote. A simple majority would pass any budget at any level. It would not be necessary to vote on all budgets at the same time, and different budgets could be structured for differing duration's of time. A proposal for deficit spending could be included in the federal budget assuming the federal government is allowed to print money. Budgets would be valid for two years and approved one year before the effective date. This stops the "hostage holding" mentality that accompanies the budgeting process in every unit of government. If not approved by the deadline, the old budget goes into effect for two more years. A positive law could be introduced at any time to authorize a budget change. A natural disaster such as an earthquake occurs; thousands are homeless and private charities are saturated. A supplement is proposes to relieve the suffering. The supplemental budget is on the electronic voting agenda in days and approved quickly. It is unlikely that a supplement to bail out a cost overrun on the super conducting supercollider or the space station would meet with equal enthusiasm.

Budgets require taxes. Citizens might agree on a level and allocation of budget, but they must still pay the piper. This means deciding whose hide the tax money comes from. With the encouragement of "democratic" politicians, the citizens believe that everyone else should pay. Better the corporations should pay, or maybe just the rich. The demagoguery exhibited by elected leaders in presenting the bill for their service make the most devious used car salesperson blush. Their rhetoric on taxing the rich, soaking the greedy corporations (who, by the way produce all of the goods and services the citizens consume), and catching the crooks that pilfer the financial system (many of whom can be found in congress and the state capitals) is loquacious and insincere. The ugly fact is that varying the sources of revenue just move the peas under the shells. The average citizen, who works and consumes, must pay the bill by consuming less. It makes sense to let these people decide. They can understand the tradeoffs given factual data. All parties are motivated to provide this data. Citizens would decide the fraction of taxes that are apportioned against enterprises, individual earnings and debt (printing money). The choices are simple. The voter would enter a percentage for each category of revenue source. The final decision is an average of the votes cast for each budget category. The percentage rate of tax (no deductions, no loopholes, etc.) becomes the basis for the government's confiscation of resources to pay the bill. The use of taxation to achieve social engineering is not allowed.

This method of dealing with complex decisions may sound too simple to be practical. *Simplicity is a great virtue.* The Congress now produces hundreds of pages of legislation per day. Most of this legislation is directed to narrow interests that are inappropriate for congress to consider. It is impossible to repeal any legislation no matter how noxious or ineffective. There is no reason for laws to be lengthy. A good law can be expressed in one paragraph. The recently passed NAFTA legislation was hundreds of pages long. It could have been less than one page if the hundreds of vested interests had not achieved their goals by inserting special provisions. A statement that all tariffs would be reduced 20% each year until they vanished would have been sufficient. Millions of dollars in legal fees can be saved. There is an ultimate elegance in simplicity. Only lawyers and politicians like complexity in matters of government. Einstein's remark about the laws of physics is equally applicable to governments, "the laws should be as simple as possible, but no simpler."

The transition from the current government to the Government will not happen quickly. Initially, the legislation and constitutional amendments would be put in place by the newly elected president and legislature. At once, no new government functions could be legislated without a 2/3 popular vote. It would take at least one year to set up the voting system. Once up and running, any individual, association or the legislature could place a government function or law on the ballot for elimination. A simple majority could eliminate government functions. A 2/3 majority would be required to restore them. Any positive law would require the same plurality for its elimination as was required for passage.

—why is the Government better?

A government is good if it helps citizens achieve their values. "Life, liberty and the pursuit of happiness" says it all. If a government satisfies a small elite who has maneuvered into control of a nations wealth, it is not good. The three axioms that the Government is founded upon helps citizens achieve their values. These axioms are "weak." They reduce to a minimum the demands on a government. If weaker axioms were posed, the result would be anarchy or authoritarianism.

The axioms require little sacrifice of ideology. A government based on religious or nationalistic dogma would be much stronger and more expansive. If an effective Government can be built on such simple and universally accepted principles, then there is no reason why the design cannot be accepted and implemented. The key to success is the overthrow of the vested interests, not the victory of either Meld or Egon principles. Professional politicians do not want this fact known. The profession of politics is no longer needed, except perhaps to resolve disputes in recreational activities such as baseball and hockey.

Axiom 1 prevents government from interfering with citizen's actions that do not harm others. This is equivalent to raising the status of negative law to the highest priority. Negative law provides stability in civil society. Melds may prefer a more dominant central authority, but they are free to pursue their dogma at lower levels of government. They can build on local successes by expanding as consensus is broadened. Whatever dogma the proselytizing group might encompass, that group could hope and dream of converting the entire nation to their faith. The only constraint Government places on proselytizing is that it proceeds from the bottom up, not the top down. This process prevents a tyranny of the majority while allowing society to drift into more dogmatic or authoritarian regimes if they universally prefer. It is unlikely that small, value homogeneous groups will prevail in perpetrating tyrannies if they are prevented from dominating a central government with political treachery.

Axiom 2 requires that the government take those actions necessary to prevent citizen or glabs from doing physical *or economic* harm to another unless that harm results from a prior voluntarily obligation.

Meld and Egon will persist with ideological differences. The Government assures both can express their values. Both groups are now manipulated by politicians and special interests for purposes which have no relationship to either's values. Everyone will gain by making positive law harder to enact. Government associations present sophistic arguments based on Meld or Egon principles to support vested interest legislation. The results of such legislation never match the projected outcomes.

The Government provides freedom for Melds to start grass root movements in any political jurisdiction. These movements, when successful, satisfy their craving for authority and togetherness. Any displeased Egon is free to move to another jurisdiction more to their liking. Changing residence to achieve value satisfaction has associated costs. The alternatives presented by monstrous central governments are far more costly. The Government allows Meld and Egon to satisfy their values. A stable society can not tolerate those that demand the sacrifice of another citizen's life and happiness. The virus of instability is found in the vested interests that manipulate governments in order to transfer wealth from citizens to themselves. This was the major defect of the Soviet Socialists and it is rapidly becoming the terminal cancer of American society.

Economic efficiencies created by the Government would be enormous. The elimination of pork barrel politics, inefficient public works projects, fraudulent transfers of public wealth, and major projects that most citizens don't want would be reduced or eliminated. The increased visibility into the law making process quickly exposes the duplicity in motives that drive legislation today. Mechanisms used to fraudulently transfer citizens' wealth to non-productive segments of society can be eliminated.

The *uniform* and *consistent* enforcement of negative law eliminates many of the tensions and conflicts created by the perpetual pleading for privilege. If the high court does its job of assuring the uniform enforcement of negative law, then the continued request for exemption would vanish. The pleaders for special privilege would realize the futility of requesting such blatant gratuities. Positive law is enacted by plebiscite and at the lowest level of government organization. This destroys the leverage of groups pleading special need for receiving confiscated wealth. Most of the pleaders for wealth transfer would be embarrassed to go before their local townspeople requesting these gifts. Instead of expending such energies on lobbying governments, they could turn to more productive tasks such as generating wealth or public begging. It is amusing to contemplate the reaction of Louisiana voters to a request from millionaire sugar farmers for $100 million in sugar subsidies.

Governments exhibit intellectual inertia and a propensity to ignore facts. If a piece of legislation does not produce the announced results, it never gets changed. How many laws has congress repealed? The plebiscite makes it much easier for the citizens to reverse their mistakes. Instead of electing leaders every few years, and hoping that they will meet their verbal commitments (which they seldom do), the citizens could immediately re-evaluate a piece of law that wasn't achieving the desired results. Instead of throwing the bastards out and getting a carbon copy in return, citizens could quickly and efficiently correct their own mistakes.

—the future

The arguments that prove the Government is better are logical and compelling. The critical thinker must ask what the negatives are. If this is such a good idea, why hasn't it been tried before? The answer is twofold. First, the technology to support the information transfers necessary to implement the Government have not been available. Politicians have been the information brokers of human society. They charge a high price for this service. With available data processing and communications technology, this service is simply not required. An analogy is the emergence of discount stock brokers who operate from touch tone telephones instead of human dialogue. They eliminated the middle man who performed the service but raked quite a bit off the top as the money flowed by. Society does not need or want politicians re interpreting facts and making judgments. Money and misery is saved. Another buggy-whip profession is eliminated. The job potential for politicians is as gloomy as that of nuclear weapon designers.

The second factor that makes the Government a timely concept is the rapid improvements in education and information availability. Much anguish is caused by the government's educational system failing to meet the needs of an expanding knowledge based economy. Citizens today know more about their environment and circumstance than ever before. They are in a better position to make reasoned judgments about government policies. Citizens have adopted new and effective educational techniques. The glabs who operate the government's education system have fiercely resisted these techniques. The middle man politician is no longer needed or wanted. Citizens in America today are capable of making all decisions that their governments have monopolized. The Government provides a mechanism for correcting errors; this is more than can be said for existing governments. The Government is not a brilliant new idea; it is an inevitable evolution of human society made possible by communications and data processing technology. The so-called "democratic" governments have become corrupt and inefficient. Any alternative that avoids more authoritarian influence is preferable. America and Europe are not far behind the Peoples Republic of China in assembling the authoritarian forces that will destroy their economies and the values of their citizens.

A political and academic elite has seized control of America's governments. These autocrats are displaying an inexcusable arrogance of power. The excuse for expanding government is always couched in terms of providing benefits to an ill defined but deserving group. The promised benefits never materialize. The poor do not get richer. The students do not get smarter. The streets are not safer. The "vigorous efforts" to cut pork barrel programs only nibble at the ankles of the leviathan.

Citizens elect political leaders. Voters must choose from a mob of power hungry despots. Elected leaders do not respond to their constituents. The majority of citizens oppose the laws passed by congress and the state legislatures. Citizens only hear the politician's position on *issues; principles* are seldom discussed. The voter's sense of compassion and fairness is twisted into perverse laws that transfer wealth and power from individuals to the government.

When debate focuses on *issues* rather than *principles*, politicians avoid taking a position that will alienate voters. The clever politician will create irrelevant issues, such as the war on drugs and term limits, to divert attention from the inexorable growth in government.

A self-serving political elite seeks power and wealth without regard to civil society. When a social order disintegrates to this sorry state of affairs, the result is a society that transfers wealth from a diminishing cadre of *producers* to an eve-growing mob of *takers*.

A crisis of confidence in government has been created by the unbridled arrogance of the political elite. This crisis is causing a political restructuring in America. New political philosophies are emerging around citizens own values and the technical and demographic realities of a modern society. Allegiance to established political parties is evaporating. Political attitudes are no longer established by the once-pure visions of liberal, conservative, communist, socialist, democrat, or fascist. These monolithic political philosophies are giving way to a politics of rational self-interest. The political and academic elite that have defined America's values since the Civil War are being eroded by a citizenry that demand their values prevail over those of government.

Since World War II, the word democracy has been used to describe a form of government that emulates the American model. Literally, democracy allows a majority of voters to determine any issue under government's purview. This kind of democracy is certainly not what the founders had in mind, and is most certainly not the kind of government America has today. The essence of America's early success was the constitution, a body of law that defined the structure and method of transition for government as well as specifying limits on governments powers over the citizens. The constitution was intended as a permanent structure that could not be changed by a majority of citizens nor by their leaders. Recently, these principles have been honored more in the breach. Instead of defining a good government as "democratic", words such as *consensus* and *legitimate* are more satisfying. The word *democracy* has, like so many other expressions of political principles, been perverted to suit the ends of the political and academic elites. America was founded as a Republic!

Democracy is a flawed concept in a society that is dominated by contention for government-controlled resources. If democracy is to work, the society cannot be dedicated to *taking*. The goal of government should be consensus. Few (certainly not a majority) citizens would approve any legislation created by congress, especially if they had an opportunity to understand the consequences. The details are never discussed publicly. Laws are hundreds of pages long. Hidden in these pages are special favors to campaign contributors or pork projects that would be approved only by the beneficiaries. Compounding this legislative heresy is a judiciary that ignores constitutional constraints.

Appendix

▼

This appendix is intended to provide precise definitions of the words commonly used in political discourse, but whose definition is often muddied for reasons of "spinning" the message. Wash your mind of doublespeak.

INDIVIDUAL—A human being who is alive. Individuals are unique since two cannot occupy the same space at the same time. There are about 5.6 billion on the earth and approximately 15% are living in Europe and North America.

GROUP—A group of individuals is an abstract concept. A group of individuals is a subset, or portion of all individuals. Objectively measured characteristics define a group. The characteristics are documented so that different observers would agree that an individual was in the group.

ASSOCIATION—An association is a group of individuals. The criterion for being included in this group *is the member's acknowledgment that they are a member.* An association is not necessarily voluntary. An association can consist of the inmates of Folsom prison. The essence of an association is that the individual knows he or she is a member. If an individual does not acknowledge membership, due to ignorance or because they cannot accept reality, then they are not a member. The member may not admit, he may not want or he may not believe in the association, but in his conscious mind he knows when he is a member. It is possible to use force, drugs or deceit to make him a member, but he is not a member until he believes he is a member. Examples of groups that meet the definition of an association include a marriage, the Democratic party, the American Medical Association and residents of Palo Alto.

CHARTER—An association must have a charter. A charter can be oral or contained in a written document. A charter defines the following characteristics of the association:

1. Goals—what is the association trying to achieve, if anything?

2. Rules of behavior for members

3. Sanctions taken by the associations' members if an individual member's behavior is not compliant with the association's charter.

4. Constraints on membership.

Association charters vary in level of detail, consistency, and precision of language. A government has a charter defined by a constitution and body of law, often with much historical clarification. A small business might have no written charter, but a clearer view of its goals and constraints.

FORCE—Force is the application, or the credible threat of application, of uninvited discomfort to one individual by another. Accidents or disease can lead to uninvited discomfort. Force is different because another purposefully directs it to one individual. While tools can be used to distance the force applicant and applicee, the effect is the same. Force is willful, the result of effort by an individual. Force applicants can work through an association, but the application of force is an individual's decision. The three manifestations of force are:

1.Physical force is the willful use of matter and energy by one individual to harm or constrain another individual. Physical force can range from murder to a shove. Other types of force can be successful only with the credible threat of physical force.

2.Confiscating possessions is more popular than Type 1 force in "civilized" societies.

3.Denying an individual a good, a service or a right (to be defined later) is the third type of force. The siege of a city denies access to food. This technique was used effectively early in human history. The current use of the embargo is less effective because of technical problems, but is conducted in the same spirit.

NATION—A nation is a portion of the planet earth. The "commons" concept is popular in international convention and requires that some territory be shared for purposes of navigation (oceans and space). A nation is, by current international conventions, a solid angle segment of the earth extending into the atmosphere but not into space. The solid angle constitutes predominantly landmasses, but typically includes some surrounding oceans. The boundaries are usually contiguous but not necessarily so. Nation defines real estate; not the individuals inhabiting the nation. Two or more associations can dispute national boundaries. A nation can include "commons" such as the right to access oceans and space. Nations often defend the access to "commons" as vigorously as they do borders. Nations are a convenience for generals and politicians. Nations result from association charters.

GOVERNMENT—A government is an association whose charter provides for the *exclusive* use of force to enforce the charters' constraints on individual member's behavior. The government's charter usually defines national boundaries as its domain. Cooperative hierarchies of governments are common. Each level of government defines a charter that allocates force exclusivity so as not to create conflict with other units of government. Federal, state, county, city, and other government units share force exclusivity. These overlapping units of governments insure full employment for politicians and bureaucrats.

CONSTITUTION/LAW—Law is the government's charter. There are two different kinds of law, as pointed out by F. A. Hayek . "*That practically all rules of just conduct are negative in the sense that they normally impose no positive duties on any one, unless he has incurred such duties by his* own *actions, is a feature that has again and again, as though it were a new discovery, been pointed out, but scarcely ever systematically investigated.*" Negative law allows individuals to engage in certain activities free of interference from other individuals. Negative law is applied consistently to all citizens, or selectively applied to certain staff of the government or other privileged groups. The Bill of Rights in the U.S. constitution is negative law. Negative laws are more fundamental to social stability and for that reason is often in a separate document, called a constitution. A constitution is more protected from changes than legislated law. Positive law requires or prohibits specific acts that citizens might undertake or shun voluntarily. Examples include paying taxes, crossing streets at the corner, smoking in restaurants, obtaining licenses, and so on. Negative law protects the individual from force applied by other individuals, including government staff. Positive law requires specific behavior from an individual (thou shalt and thou shalt not, as opposed to thou may). Force or the credible threat of force is used to assure compliant behavior. Positive and negative law are so different that it would be better if described by different words.

CITIZENS—Citizens are that group of individuals whom the government's charter defines as those subject to the use of force by the government. Citizens are defined by place of residence, race, birthplace, or other characteristics that governments choose. Since government has the exclusive charter for use of force, the citizen must accept the government's demands. The government is unique since it creates association members without informing them of their membership. Force exclusivity makes this high-handed technique possible. Individuals only join associations they choose unless force is used. The government can define a group of individuals as members and apply force to acquaint them with their membership.

GOODS—Goods are the material items, services and information which individual's consume. An item or activity becomes a good only by consumption or assigning ownership for consumption.

RESOURCE—A resource is any material item or information that individuals value except goods. Resources are not consumed. Often the same commodity is both a good and a resource, for example gold and oats. The distinction is important for defining government's role in establishing ownership. Only individuals consume. Another word for owned goods and resources is wealth. The value of goods and resources is time dependent. The value of goods decline as an individual must wait to consume them. Economists introduce the notion of a discount rate to reflect this fact.

OWN—Owning associates a good or resource to an individual or an association. The state of owning can come about in a variety of ways. The government's charter is often heavy on the details of ownership. Conflicts over ownership are resolved by behavior that respects the law, by force or by consumption. *Establishing and enforcing rules of ownership is the primary mechanism by which governments avoid anarchy*. Civil society cannot exist without rules of ownership and the effective enforcement of these rules by government. Effective ownership must include *control* over the item owned as well as title that allows sale or transfer.

ENTERPRISE—An enterprise is an association whose charter includes the goals of applying members' efforts toward the creation or accumulation of goods or resources. An enterprise can engage in production of goods or resources, brokerage, arbitrage and fraud. Production provides goods, services, knowledge or information and adds value to resources. Brokerage is buying and selling for others' accounts. Arbitrage is buying and selling for ones own account. Many enterprises use fraud to accumulate wealth. Some of these fraudulent enterprises are illegal. (Fraud is defined later.)

RIGHT—A right is the assurance to an individual that he may engage in certain activities without interference by others. Governments create rights. The most basic rights are implemented through negative law. This definition of rights excludes "natural rights" that are supposed to befall individuals because of some supernatural power or preconceived natural order of things. *For a right to be meaningful, it must be enforced. Since* government *has the exclusive use of* force, *it follows that* rights *have substance only when incorporated into a* government charter. Historically, rights have been considered negative law and defined in constitutional law. In recent governments, rights have included the guarantee that each citizen may consume certain goods. The government can enforce such rights only by transferring wealth. Governments must confiscate some wealth to enforce negative law. The police, judges and jailers must be paid. Resources are required to build jails and police stations. Wealth can be generated for these purposes only by use of the force exclusivity. Even the most loyal citizens might not volunteer their wealth to pay police and jailers. Examples make this important distinction clear. The right to "free speech" implies that an individual or association can discuss, publish or broadcast most any material if it falls within broad norms of acceptability. This is negative law. The right to health care requires wealth transfers or compulsory services; this is positive law. Both are rights. Rights can become contradictory. One individual exercising a right may infringe upon another individual's right. Much civil and criminal law addresses the resolution of conflicting rights. The profession of law has profited enormously by the government's construction of complex and contradictory rights. The fewer laws and the more simply expressed, the less the chance of conflict.

MONEY—A token item that that most citizens accept in exchange for goods and resources and is relatively permanent in the environments that it is used. Money is often defined in a government's charter. This is not necessary. Scarce commodities or paper defining commitments of individuals or enterprises have been used as money without government sanction. Paper that commits ownership of enterprises (associations) or resources (commodities and land) are used by civil society. Derivatives that represent paper secured by the underlying asset are used to facilitate risk distribution. Examples include insurance policies, commodities futures, puts and calls on securities, or securities that reflect ownership of bundled obligations such as home mortgages. Civil society can devise methods of creating workable money without government intervention. Governments are loath to give up the exclusive charter to print money because this allows the dilution of money's value. This trick effectively transfers wealth to government-sponsored activities. Money provides a convenience for trading resources or their paper derivatives by providing a measurable and standard unit of exchange. Governments learned that they could extract a hefty price for monopolizing this service.

EFFORT The purposeful activity of an individual that

1. CREATES Transforms resources into goods or add value to resources.

2. CONSUMES Consumption of goods.

3. ADVOCATES Attempting to change the behavior of other individuals.

POLITICAL EFFORT is advocacy directed towards or resulting in changing the charter or staffing of an association. This definition is important for governments, but is applicable to civil associations as well. If an association does not have a force exclusivity clause in its charter, changes in staff or charter are of little interest to those outside the association. Some associations ("criminal" ones such as the Mafia or street gangs) incorporate clauses allowing force to be used by the members, but they do not claim force exclusivity. These criminal associations run afoul of the law, but do not challenge the government's force exclusivity. Only revolutions or wars challenge force exclusivity. Political effort in these associations can affect non-members. Governments tolerate such "criminal" associations (witness Italy's historical tolerance of organized crime) as long as they do not seriously infringe the government's charter, particularly force exclusivity. Politicians in office often associate with criminals but not with revolutionaries.

COMMERCE—Commerce is the voluntary exchange of goods, resources, effort or money by individuals or associations.

CONFLICT—One individual can create a conflict with another by exerting an effort to change his actions, ownership status or values. It is always difficult to know why a conflict arises unless it involves ownership of wealth. Most conflicts arise over perceptions or actions.

VOLUNTARY effort is undertaken without the application or credible threat of force.

CONTRACT A voluntary agreement among individuals or associations that include obligations, time when obligations are to be consummated and penalties for failure to meet obligations. A body of law may make implicit terms of timeliness and penalties for failing to meet contractual obligations. An essential role of government is to ensure, under threat of force, that private contracts are honored. *Rules of contract are closely associated with creating ownership, and are hence essential to prevent anarchy and allow civil society to flourish.* The threat of force is essential to assure contracts are honored.

VALUES are mental processes of individuals that effect their efforts. Only individuals have (own) values, and they can change with the passage of time. Associations do not have values, but they can advocate values and require their members to advocate values. Values are relevant only when they effect individual action or effort. Values are a "hidden variable" in the science of government. Values are important to society because of the behavior that results. **The values verbalized by an individual are not necessarily the values upon which that individuals acts.** Examples include the actions of many politicians and religious leaders. "Value duplicity" is common, particularly among politicians. Values can only be inferred from behavior and commitments, not verbal or written proclamations.

FRAUD The potential for fraud is the reason for contract law. The government must resolve conflicts resulting from fraud. When two or more individuals or associations enter into a contract, they agree to meet commitments of transferring wealth or effort (obligations) to others within specified times and conditions. When one party to the contract fails to meet his commitments and the other party is not in breach, then the violating party is engaging in fraud. The intentions or the circumstances of the individual committing fraud are irrelevant. Fraud does not imply "intent." An important function of government is to use force to remedy breaches of contract. The method a government uses to stop fraud is important to civil society. Law may allow a contract to be oral if verifiable with witnesses. Politicians often make oral contracts with citizens in exchange for votes (and the politician's salary), but then fail to deliver. Should laws that provide remedies for defrauded parties be applied in these cases? The losses can be substantial.

0-595-26922-2

www.ingramcontent.com/pod-product-compliance
Lightning Source LLC
Chambersburg PA
CBHW061258280526
45784CB00002B/801